IPS

Supplying Repression

U.S. Support for Authoritarian Regimes Abroad

Michael T. Klare
Cynthia Arnson

with Delia Miller and Daniel Volman
Foreword by Richard Falk

✣ 1981 Michael T. Klare and Cynthia Arnson and the Institute for Policy Studies.

Published by the Institute for Policy Studies.

Copies of this book are available from the Institute for Policy Studies, 1901 Q Street N.W., Washington, D.C. 20009 or The Transnational Institute, Paulus Potterstraat 20, 1071 DA, Amsterdam, Holland.

Revised First Printing, 1981
Second Printing, 1978
First Printing, 1977

ISBN 0-89758-024-9 paper
ISBN 0-89758-033-8 cloth

TABLE OF CONTENTS

LIST OF TABLES

vi

FOREWORD

Although expected, it still seems shocking. Ronald Reagan has made it evident from the outset of his presidency that every anti-Communist government, no matter how despicable its internal policies, is henceforth to be treated as a friend of the United States. Virtually since Inauguration Day, the White House has made a point of hosting leaders of repressive regimes, starting with the notorious Chun Doo-Hwan of South Korea and Roberto Viola of Argentina. Furthermore, a new positive approach has unashamedly been proclaimed with respect to such international pariahs as South Africa and Chile. More spectacularly, Washington has adopted an openly interventionist policy toward the struggle in El Salvador and has hinted broadly of a willingness to destabilize "unfriendly" governments in Angola and Nicaragua. Such developments reveal unmistakably the onset of a new era of blatant counterinsurgency.

In this respect, Alexander Haig's declaration of war against terrorism is, in its essence, a campaign agaist the forces of revolutionary nationalism in the Third World. These are the forces that threaten United States positions of dominance and privilege around the world. Popular victories over dictatorship in Iran and Nicaragua in 1978-79 convinced mainstream American policymakers that despite "the lessons of Vietnam," it was essential to return to their counterinsurgency drawing boards. Of course, this "resolve"—to use a word that has a strong appeal for the *Commentary* breed of cold war revitalists—antedated Reagan. Ideas about "unleashing the CIA," supplementing the Green Berets with the Rapid Deployment Force, and new regional commitments by the United States to avoid "another Iran" in the Persian Gulf and "another Nicaragua" in the Caribbean were prevalent in the late Carter period. Indeed, Michael Klare and Cynthia Arnson significantly document here the extent to which an increase in the American role as exporter of the tools of repression paralleled Jimmy Carter's human rights diplomacy. Such a demonstration recalls and further vindicates Klare's daring analysis of more than a decade ago in *War Without End*

(Knopf, 1972), depicting a *structural* commitment by the United States to counterinsurgency, that is, one that inevitably follows from the pattern of interests and relationships that joins the United States to the Third World and that expresses itself in the form of a permanent war against the various manifestations of revolutionary nationalism. Only the tactics vary, not the essential confrontation. The Reagan/Haig approach, with its abandonment of human rights pretensions, makes manifest what had earlier been more hidden, and temporarily—because of public disaffection after Vietnam—less militarist.

There are some encouraging signs that the elaborate effort by the bipartisan leadership of this country to erase the Vietnam experience from our collective memory has so far largely failed. Public opinion polls indicate a remarkably low level of support for the El Salvador intervention. Despite even an official "white paper" allegedly documenting the Soviet/Cuban connection only a miniscule 2% of Americans favor, as of March 1981, sending troops to help the junta out and less than 20% favor either economic or military aid. These are remarkably low levels of support for an interventionary policy whose rationale has been so carefully nurtured at the highest levels of government.

Yet, a strong democratic mandate has rarely been deemed necessary by the power-wielders in Washington. It is enough if the public shuts up, minds its own consumerist business, and leaves the tactics of imperial defense where it belongs—namely, in the professional hands of leaders and bureaucrats. And so, whether popular or not, we can expect these interventionary policies of support for repression to go on, at least until effectively opposed by a strong social movement in this country.

One of the vital tools of active opposition is persuasive information. Contrary to liberal illusion, formal freedoms do not assure the quality of information and analysis needed for an alert citizenry. Media bias, secrecy, special-interest lobbying, and the black arts of "disinformation" are a formidable array of obstacles. For these reasons it requires ingenuity, perseverance, and a clarity of will to gather and present information in a manner that is at once compelling and mobilizing. Michael Klare has been a pioneer researcher at the information frontier of the imperial/war system for years indicating the viability and relevance of such an enterprise even in our kind of "closed society." This volume, written in collaboration with Cynthia Arnson, updates and extends his valuable study of U.S. support for authoritarian governments. Their analysis enables us to get beyond slogans and to grasp the organic links between training, repressive tactics, and the anguish of torture victims. This portrayal makes it unmistakably clear that the United States is and has been all along a knowing senior partner of repression on a global scale. And, indeed, the new emerging Reagan foreign policy based on an all-oceans American-led alliance of right-wing governments boldly acknowledges our dependence on these repressive regimes and their dependence on us for the latest "off-the-shelf" knowhow and hardware.

More fully and convincingly than anywhere else, Klare and Arnson, with dispassionate precision and attention to detail, depict the profiles of this distinctively American Gulag. Let us hope that our response as readers will be less dispassionate, that we will begin to insist that our government stay out of the repression trade. Without such an insistence we will find ourselves as citizens indicted as co-conspirators in this central imperial effort to crush the struggles of Third World peoples to control their own social, political, and cultural destiny.

Richard Falk
Albert G. Milbank Professor
of International Law and Practice
Princeton University

ACKNOWLEDGEMENTS

This edition of *Supplying Repression* covers many more program areas and contains far more information than the first edition, published in 1977 by the Field Foundation (and later reprinted by the Institute for Policy Studies). To obtain additional material for this edition, we consulted with hundreds of scholars, researchers and human rights activists in this country and abroad. Many of these people also contributed in a significant way to our understanding and analysis of the issu ں raised in this study.

While space limitations and discretion prevent us from identifying all of the people who who assisted in the preparation of this edition, we wish to express particular gratitude to: Max Holland of the Center for International Policy; Sherman Carroll of Amnesty International in London; Stephanie Grant of Amnesty International in Washington; Steve Wright of the Richardson Institute, University of Lancaster; Chris Root and Ted Lockwood of the Washington Office on Africa; Peter Lock of the Working Group on Armaments and Underdevelopment of the University of Hamburg; Ann Laurent of the Argentine Commission on Human Rights; Prof. Richard Falk of Princeton University; Leslie Dunbar; Alex Knopp; Eric Prokosch; Phillip O'Neil; Cora and Peter Weiss; Roland Seeman; and the staffs of SIPRI (Stockholm International Peace Research Institute), NARMIC (National Action/Research on the Military-Industrial Complex), NACLA (the North American Congress on Latin America), the Data Center of Oakland, California, the Coalition for a New Foreign and Military Policy, Friends Committee on National Legislation, Southern Africa Committee, the Washington Office on Latin America, and the Center for National Security Studies.

Furthermore, it must be acknowledged that a project of this scope could not have been undertaken without supplementary financial assistance, and thus we are deeply grateful for the support of the Rubin Foundation, the Field Foundation, the International Foundation for Development Alternatives, the Veatch Program of the

North Shore Unitarian Church, the Car-Eth Foundation, and the Boehm Foundation for enabling us to complete this effort.

Finally, a special vote of thanks is due to all the people at I.P.S. who helped us in innumerable ways, especially Delia Miller, Daniel Volman, Steve Daggett, Bob Borosage, Saul Landau, Isabel Letelier, and Alyce Wiley.

—*Michael Klare and Cynthia Arnson*

I.

INTRODUCTION:

HUMAN RIGHTS & THE REPRESSION TRADE

After his inauguration in 1977, President Carter assured us of his "undeviating commitment" to the advancement of human rights abroad. In his first address to the United Nations, on March 17, 1977, he affirmed America's obligation to "work with our potential adversaries as well as our close friends to advance the cause of human rights." No member of the U.N., he declared, "can avoid its responsibilities to speak when torture or unwarranted deprivation occurs in any part of the world." Subsequently, he told graduating seniors at Notre Dame University that American foreign policy would henceforth "reflect our people's basic commitment to promote the cause of human rights."[1]

The moral tone of Carter's statements, while hardly absent from earlier presidential statements on foreign policy, differed substantially from that of his predecessors. For most of the post-World War II era, U.S. foreign policy had stressed the development of military links with anti-Communist governments throughout the world, irrespective of their commitment—or lack thereof—to fundamental human rights and liberties. After Vietnam, however, the American public began to question this policy, especially when it became known (through the Watergate hearings and special Senate investigations) that Washington had employed intrigue and assassination to subvert democratic governments while cooperating in the enthronement and survival of some of the world's most brutal dictatorships. As a candidate, Carter sensed that the issue of human rights tapped deep into the roots of domestic malaise over foreign adventures, and he determined to make it a conspicuous feature of his "post-Vietnam" foreign policy. In an early expression of this new approach, he told the Permanent Council of the Organization of American States that "Our values . . . require us to combat abuses of individual freedom, including those caused by political, social, and economic injustice."[2]

For the next three years, the issue of human rights figured prominently in America's foreign relations. Countries with a poor record in the human rights area were chastised by Washington, and in some cases denied access to U.S. military and economic aid. U.S. relations with the Soviet Union took a turn for the worse when Mr. Carter criticized Moscow for its persecution of dissident intellectuals. While many people praised Carter's vigorous human rights stance, others complained that it went too far—or not far enough. As time went on, however, the issue of human rights appeared less compelling as other problems—the energy crisis, the Iranian hostage takeover, Afghanistan—dominated public attention. By the beginning of 1980, human rights had ceased to be the rallying cry of the Administration, and Mr. Carter adopted a more hawkish stance in preparation for the campaign against Ronald Reagan.

Now a new Administration has taken power in Washington—one that has pledged to downgrade the importance placed on human rights in official government policy.* Said Reagan himself shortly after his election, "I don't think that you can turn away from some country because here and there they do not agree with our concept of human rights."[4]

Given this posture, it is evident that Reagan will resume U.S. arms aid to many of the countries which were formerly ineligible for such assistance on human rights

---

*"International terrorism will take the place of human rights," declared Alexander Haig, Jr. in his first press conference as Secretary of State. He went on to accuse the Soviet Union of "training, funding, and equipping" terrorist activities, and said that "an extraordinary role" for human rights could produce "distortions" in foreign policy-making.[3]

grounds. Reagan is also expected to lift the restraints imposed by President Carter on the Pentagon's Foreign Military Sales program, and to simplify procedures for private arms suppliers seeking to export weapons through the Commercial Sales program. If past experience is any indicator, these arms will flow to precisely those agencies—the military, the police, and paramilitary security organizations—which are most directly responsible for the abuses which led to the cutoffs in the first place. Accordingly, this appears an appropriate time to examine the various ways in which the United States contributes to the repressive capacities of foreign dictatorships, and to review the relative effectiveness of Carter's efforts to curb such activities.

THE CARTER POLICY: DETACHMENT OR COMPLICITY?

President Carter's approach to the human rights problem can perhaps best be described as a *juridical* outlook: when violations occurred abroad, the appropriate American response was to investigate such violations and, if the government involved was deemed responsible, to penalize it through diplomatic protests, public condemnation, and, in extreme cases, cutbacks in U.S. aid and assistance. This outlook was manifest in Carter's 1977 assertion that the Helsinki agreements endow us with "a responsibility and a legal right to express our disapproval of violations of human rights,"[5] and in his decision to reduce U.S. military aid to particular violators, including Argentina, Ethiopia, and Uruguay. But while this approach had a certain intrinsic logic, it falsely suggested that human rights violations were wholly the responsibility of the foreign government involved, and that the United States was somehow detached or disconnected from such abuses; in fact, the evidence suggests that the United States is, and has been, deeply complicit in the proliferation of repression abroad, through its military and economic support for authoritarian regimes and through *sales of repressive technology and techniques to those foreign*

3

government agencies directly responsible for political terrorism and the suppression of dissent.

To demonstrate the extent of U.S. involvement in repression, let us look at ten countries which have often been cited by Amnesty International and similar groups for consistent patterns of abuse: Argentina, Brazil, Guatemala, Indonesia, Iran, Morocco, the Philippines, South Korea, Taiwan, and Thailand. These countries are not the only ones with a poor record on human rights, but they stand out because of persistent reports of government-sanctioned torture, assassination, and arbitrary arrest.[6] In all of these countries, moreover, state security agencies have engaged in a systematic pattern of political terrorism against minorities, trade unions, clergy, and students, and other dissident groups. Furthermore, all have been *major recipients of U.S. arms and military assistance.*

Consider: Between 1976 and 1980, these ten countries received $2.3 billion in military aid and arms credits from the United States, or about one-third of all such aid awarded in this period (excluding Congressionally-mandated grants to Israel). In addition, these nations bought a staggering $13.7 billion worth of U.S. arms under the Foreign Military Sales (FMS) and Commercial Sales programs. (See Table I.) And despite President Carter's pledge to cut back on U.S. arms aid to governments which consistently violate human rights, these ten nations were scheduled to receive $395 million in grants and loans in Fiscal 1981, and to buy another $2.2 billion worth of U.S. weapons.[7]

Officially, U.S. arms programs are designed to strengthen the capacity of countries to defend themselves against *external* attack. But an examination of U.S. weapons trade data suggests that much of the equipment involved is intended for *internal* use, to control strikes and disorders and to suppress dissent. Thus recent arms deliveries to these countries have included armored cars, shotguns, tear gas, riot clubs, and other weapons unsuitable for anything other than internal political warfare. Such weapons present problems of abuse even when sold to the most democratic of governments; when sold to dictators, they almost always contribute to

TABLE I:
U.S. Military Aid and Arms Sales to Selected Human Rights Violators, Fiscal Years 1976-80[1]
(Current U.S. dollars in thousands)

Country	MAP Grants	FMS Credits	Excess Defense Articles	IMET	Total Aid	FMS Sales	Com- mercial Sales	Total Sales
Argentina	—	34,000	—	1,115	35,115	42,590	82,463	125,053
Brazil	—	43,423	—	663	44,086	41,222	68,735	109,957
Guatemala	173	1,391	—	936	2,500	15,574	3,768	19,342
Indonesia	52,996	151,200	6,512	11,516	222,224	189,633	36,845	226,478
Iran	—	—	—	—	—	6,298,435	466,274	6,764,709
Morocco	—	178,000	—	4,988	182,988	409,674	71,602	481,276
Philippines	96,531	121,500	5,325	3,445	246,801	176,492	58,252	234,744
S. Korea	61,552	1,067,500	1,177	7,568	1,137,797	2,302,506	311,255	2,613,761
Taiwan	884	151,500	—	1,540	153,924	1,882,982	251,896	2,134,878
Thailand	42,354	166,200	65,035	5,398	278,987	901,301	41,789	943,090
TOTAL	254,490	1,914,714	78,049	37,169	2,304,422	12,260,409	1,392,879	13,653,288

1. Source: U.S. Dept. of Defense, *Foreign Military Sales and Military Assistance Facts* (Washington, D.C.: 1980), and U.S. Dept. of Defense, *Security Assistance Program*, Congressional Presentation Document, Fiscal Year 1981 (Washington, D.C.: 1980).

5

repression and political terror. Thus U.S. arms were used by the Thai Border Patrol Police to massacre hundreds of students during the military coup of October 6, 1976; by the Iranian Army to kill thousands of unarmed demonstrators during the 1978 uprising against the Shah; and by Indonesian troops charged with the wholesale slaughter of civilians in occupied East Timor.

And this is only the tip of the iceberg of U.S. involvement in repression abroad. Information obtained by the authors under the Freedom of Information Act shows that U.S. firms and agencies are providing guns, equipment, training, and technical support to the police and paramilitary forces *most directly involved in the torture, assassination, and abuse of civilian dissidents.* Turning again to our ten select offenders, we find that over the past five years the United States has:

• Sold police and security forces a vast hoard of small arms and anti-riot gear, including 13,308 pistols and revolvers; 17,495 rifles and carbines; 25,649 CN and CS gas grenades; and 6,139,000 rounds of ammunition. (See Chapter 4.)

• Provided government agencies with assorted quantities of other repressive devices used to identify, track, fetter, and maim individual dissidents. Such equipment, exported under Commerce Department auspices, has included fingerprint computers, thumbscrews, leg-irons, and electronic "Shok-Batons." (See Chapter 5.)

• Supplied $20.5 million in police gear and training under the International Narcotics Control Program. Although such grants are restricted by law to the support of drug-control programs, the General Accounting Office has found that they often go to units which engage in anti-dissident as well as anti-narcotics programs. (See Chapter 2.)

• Trained 6,013 officers and soldiers from these countries at military schools in the United States and at U.S. bases abroad. While most of these students took courses in standard combat operations—infantry, armor, etc.—a substantial number were enrolled in special programs on internal security which featured courses on such topics as Urban Counterinsurgency, Military Police

Operations, and Security Management. (See Chapter 3.)

All this paints a very different picture from that suggested by Mr. Carter's quasi-judicial posture on human rights. Rather than sitting in detached judgment over incidents of abuse occurring elsewhere, *the United States stands at the supply end of a pipeline of repressive technology that extends to many of the world's most authoritarian regimes.* This pipeline has been operating steadily since the end of World War II, continually gaining outlets to more and more countries. And despite everything said about human rights during the Carter Administration, this pipeline remains fully operational today—and ready to accommodate the new upsurge in repression exports promised by the Reagan Administration.[8]

Under U.S. law, any person who assists a felon in committing a crime—say by supplying the weapon used in an assassination—is considered an *accessory* to the crime and can be punished accordingly. And while the same principle is not always applicable to international law, logic suggests that any government which assists another in the abuse of human rights—say by supplying the weapons used for assassination—is an accessory to such offenses and should be condemned accordingly. So long as Washington supplies repressive technology to foreign dictators, the United States will remain a party to any violations of human rights committed in those countries.

The United States is not, of course, the only nation involved in the supply of military and police hardware to repressive regimes in the Third World. Other Western powers, including France, Great Britain and Belgium, have long traded in such commodities, while the Soviet Union and its allies (particularly Czechoslovakia and East Germany) have also become active suppliers. Indeed, when we examine this phenomenon from a global perspective, it is evident that U.S. sales constitute but a part of what can best be called the *international repression trade*—the global commerce in police weapons, prison gear, torture devices, and other hardware and techniques used by authoritarian governments to suppress dissent. And while this topic clearly merits

7

consideration as an *international* issue (an approach we adopt in Appendix I to this study), our concern here is with the *U.S. component* of this trade—both because of America's long-standing leadership in such commerce (industry sources confirm that the United States is the world's leading supplier of police and prison hardware), and because, as Americans, we feel our responsibility lies in scrutinizing what our own government and institutions are doing to promote or retard the observance of fundamental human rights.

Although it cannot be denied that the United States is involved in the sale of repressive technology abroad, some analysts have attempted to suggest that such involvement is a peripheral or unintentional facet of U.S. arms policy. But the historical record, and the data presented in these pages, suggests otherwise. As we shall demonstrate, the supply of repressive hardware to authoritarian Third World regimes is a *consistent and intentional* characteristic of U.S. foreign policy. Under the guise of "national security"—that ever-elastic excuse for U.S. commitments abroad—the United States has systematically strengthened the internal security capabilities of Third World governments considered hospitable to U.S. influence and investment.

THE "NATIONAL SECURITY" SYNDROME

While the scope of this monograph does not permit us to review the evolution and intent of U.S. military aid policies in detail, it is important that we discuss some of the main lines of their development and growth.

In the early Cold War period, under the policy of "containment," the United States sought to enhance the self-defense capacities of friendly governments on the periphery of the Soviet Union and China, as well as in Third World areas thought to be ripe for Communist subversion. The principal vehicle for such support was the Military Assistance Program (MAP), established by the Mutual Security Act of 1951. Typically, MAP aid included support for internal security forces, but in general the

8

emphasis was on developing conventional forces capable of withstanding an external military threat. In Latin America, for instance, Washington provided warships, patrol planes, and other weapons designed to enhance hemispheric defense against a hypothetical Soviet naval attack. All told, the United States gave away $26.5 billion worth of arms under the MAP program between 1946 and 1961, with the bulk of these grants going to the "forward defense countries" on the border of China and the Soviet Union.[9]

With the triumph of the Cuban Revolution in 1959, Washington was forced to reexamine its military aid policies. By defeating Batista's U.S.-armed conventional forces, Castro demonstrated that aid programs emphasizing defense against external attack did not necessarily afford protection from internal guerrilla warfare. As the threat of such "national liberation wars" loomed more prominent, Washington began placing more emphasis on developing "counterinsurgency" capabilities in friendly Third World countries to combat indigenous guerrilla armies. Then, when President Kennedy took office in 1961, counterinsurgency became the *principal* focus of MAP assistance to most Third World countries, while external defense was relegated to a decidedly secondary position. Thus, as noted by Professor Edwin Lieuwen of the University of New Mexico in a 1969 Senate study, "the basis for military aid to Latin America abruptly shifted from hemispheric defense to internal security, from the protection of coastlines and from antisubmarine warfare to defense against Castro-communist guerrilla warfare."[10]

The Kennedy Administration's preoccupation with counterinsurgency and internal security naturally resulted in increased levels of support for foreign police and paramilitary forces. In a discussion of the new priorities, then Defense Secretary Robert S. McNamara told a Congressional subcommittee that the aim of the MAP program in Latin America "is to aid, where necessary, in the continued development of indigenous military and paramilitary forces capable of providing, in conjunction with the police and other security forces, the needed domestic security."[11] In keeping with this approach, Kennedy established within the Agency for

International Development (AID) a special bureau, the Office of Public Safety (OPS), to furnish aid directly to the police forces of friendly governments in the "developing" countries. Under this program, the United States provided some $200 million worth of tear gas, firearms, and related equipment to foreign police and security agencies over the ensuing decade. (See Chapter 2.)

The shift of emphasis from external defense to counterinsurgency was perhaps most visible in Southeast Asia, where the United States assumed a major role in the struggle against revolutionary guerrilla armies. Although this commitment ultimately led to the direct involvement of U.S. combat troops, the process began with a concerted U.S. effort to build up South Vietnam's internal security capabilities. Between 1962 and 1975, the United States furnished $16.2 billion in arms aid to Vietnamese military and paramilitary forces, and additional hundreds of millions of dollars in CIA funds (the total amount is secret) to the Vietnamese police. American funds were also used to establish paramilitary terror organizations, to build new prison facilities, and to construct the notorious "Provincial Interrogation Centers" where political suspects were brought for questioning and torture.[12] Despite such backing, the South Vietnamese Army never proved capable of overcoming the National Liberation Front and Washington was forced to bring in over 500,000 of our own troops in a futile attempt to save the Saigon regime.

The failure of intervention abroad and mounting political turmoil at home led to another reappraisal of military policy. Washington's first concern was to find some formula that would insure the survival of other threatened regimes without requiring direct intervention by combat troops. This led in 1969 to adoption of the Nixon Doctrine. The new policy called for a greater self-defense effort on the part of allies, backed up by increased aid and technical support from the United States. The doctrine's operative clause held that: "in cases of [non-nuclear] aggression, we shall furnish military and economic assistance when requested, but we shall look to the nation directly threatened to assume the primary

responsibility of providing the manpower for its

defense."[13]

To carry out America's side of the bargain, the Nixon administration asked Congress to provide a substantial increase in MAP appropriations. Speaking on behalf of the new doctrine, then Secretary of Defense Melvin Laird told the House Appropriations Committee in 1970 that:

The basic policy of decreasing direct U.S. military involvement cannot be successful unless we provide our friends and allies . . . with the material assistance necessary to insure the most effective possible contribution by the manpower they are willing and able to commit to their own and the common defense. Many of them simply do not command the resources or technical capablities to assume greater responsibility for their own defense without such assistance. The challenging objectives of our new policy can, therefore, best be achieved when each partner does its share and contributes what it can to the common effort. In the majority of cases, this means indigenous manpower organized into properly equipped and well-trained armed forces with the help of material, training, technology, and specialized military skills furnished by the United States.[14]

On this basis, U.S. military aid jumped from an average of $2.4 billion per year during the Kennedy and Johnson administrations to approximately $4 billion annually during the Nixon era. And when, in the wake of the Vietnam disaster, Congress began to balk at ever-increasing MAP requests, Mr. Nixon (and later President Ford) ordered substantial increases in military *sales,* to insure that the flow of arms to friendly regimes would continue without interruption.

Although the Nixon Doctrine was originally seen as a purely *reactive* policy, designed to rationalize the American exodus from Southeast Asia, it soon assumed a more aggressive role. Believing that America's overseas interests would be placed in jeopardy by doubts of American intervention, U.S. leaders sought to build up the counterinsurgency forces of selected Third World powers in order to create a surrogate "police" presence in threatened areas. This strategy was most actively pursued in the Persian Gulf, where some of America's most valuable overseas interests—the oil supplies in Saudi Arabia, Iran, and Kuwait—are located. In order to safeguard access to this vital resource, Washington attempted to convert Iran and Saudi Arabia into regional military powers capable of overcoming any insurgent threat to existing Gulf regimes. As related by Deputy Assistant Secretary of Defense James H. Noyes, the National Security Council concluded in 1969 that "primary responsibility for peace and stability [in the Gulf] would henceforth fall on the states of the region," with the United States providing arms and equipment "in the spirit of the Nixon doctrine."[15]

This aggressive thrust was manifest in another aspect of the Nixon Doctrine: the increase in U.S. support for Third World *police* forces. Arguing that future disasters of the Vietnam type could be prevented by effective police action at the very beginning of an insurgency, administration officials sought increased funding for the overseas programs of the Office of Public Safety. (See Chapter 2.)

As in the case of all earlier administrations, Nixon's staff rarely distinguished between more or less authoritarian governments when dispensing arms and assistance. This was not because U.S. leaders were indifferent to the authoritarian character of many of the regimes they were supporting, but because the priorities of the moment—containment under Truman and Eisenhower, counterinsurgency under Kennedy, "Vietnamization" under Nixon—took precedence over all other considerations. In defending this outlook, officials have always insisted that "national security" is predicated on the existence of an interlocking network of anticommunist alliances. While some of the nations in these networks are ruled by undemocratic governments, their participation is considered necessary to the survival of the system as a whole, and therefore Washington cannot afford the "luxury" of withholding military assistance to any of them.

This principle was advanced with particular eloquence by Henry Kissinger, who was often called upon to defend U.S. assistance to repressive regimes during his tenure as Secretary of State. Testifying on aid to the then ruling junta in Greece, for instance, he told the Senate Foreign Relations Committee in 1974 that:

> *Given Greece's strategic role on the southern flank of NATO, it has been the judgment of the administration to submit these requests even though the political form, the domestic structure of Greece, is not one which we would commend... Military relations with Greece should not be considered approbation of the form of government in Greece. It is based on our interpretation of the American national interest and of the alliance interest in the defense of the Mediterranean.*[16]

An even more supple defense of support for authoritarian regimes was advanced by then Secretary of Defense James Schlesinger, who commented on the varieties of "free world" governments in testimony before the Senate Appropriations Committee:

> *I do believe... that there are nations with which we share common political ideals, [principally] the high valuation of individual freedom and of just laws impartially, consistently applied. On the other hand, many nations fall, for one reason or another, outside that general grouping. With respect to those, we may be extremely critical of their internal systems and even uncomfortable about the intimacy of our relations with them. Nevertheless, [these countries] one way or another can contribute to international or regional stability [and thus] it is frequently in our interest to provide a degree of support to supplement self-defense capabilities and efforts.*[17]

Although this principle is deeply ingrained in American elites' foreign policy outlook, significant segments of the American public rejected such rationales in the wake of the Vietnam fiasco. Religious and humanitarian organizations began campaigning for a more vigorous U.S. effort in promoting human rights abroad, and for the termination of aid to the more **13** repressive regimes, including those in South Korea, the Philippines, Iran, Taiwan, and Brazil. The bloody overthrow of the Allende government in 1973, and its replacement by the brutal Pinochet dictatorship, gave added impetus to this campaign. Increasingly, the human rights advocates turned to Congress and by 1974 began to have an impact on Capitol Hill. The Foreign Assistance Act of 1974, passed on December 30, embraced, for the first time, the principle that aid should be denied to governments which engage in systematic violations of human rights. Specifically, the 1974 Act amended the Foreign Assistance Act of 1961 (the governing legislation in this area) by adding Section 502B, which begins with the statement:

It is the sense of Congress that, except in extraordinary circumstances, the President shall substantially reduce or terminate security assistance to any government which engages in a consistent pattern of gross violations of internationally recognized human rights, including torture or cruel, inhuman or degrading treatment or punishment; prolonged detention without charges; or other flagrant denials of the right to life, liberty, and the security of the person.

The 1974 Act also included a ban on the provision of aid or training to foreign police forces, thus causing the dissolution of the Office of Public Safety (but not, as we shall see, the termination of arms deliveries to police agencies abroad).

During the Nixon and Ford administrations, most action regarding human rights was initiated by Congress. But when Jimmy Carter became President in January 1977, the White House assumed the vanguard role. For the most part, Carter confined his human rights activism to the release of statements criticizing this or that regime for alleged violations. Carter also acknowledged, at least in principle, the relationship between U.S. arms exports and the proliferation of repression abroad. Shortly after taking office, he ordered cutbacks in military aid to a few dictatorships as a penalty for conspicuous human rights violations, and imposed some restraints on the sale of police-type weapons to several other repressive regimes. But Carter never questioned the national security justification that had governed U.S. arms exports for most of the post-World War II period, and thus he was *precluded from the start* from dismantling the repression pipeline that helped sustain so many authoritarian governments.

Ultimately, the biggest problem with Carter's approach was its definition of human rights as another "concern" that had to be harmonized with a long list of other foreign policy objectives. As President Carter explained in a 1978 meeting with human rights activists, "Often, a choice that moves us toward one goal tends to move us away from another goal. Seldom do circumstances permit me or you to take actions that are wholly satisfactory to everyone."[18] So long as the country in question was of no strategic significance and did not raise any of these other foreign policy considerations, human rights might be accorded primacy with a consequent reduction in U.S. assistance. But if, on the other hand, a given country was considered to be of strategic importance, human rights was usually relegated to the bottom of the list. Thus Carter cut military assistance to a few small countries in South and Central America (Guatemala, Nicaragua, Uruguay), while maintaining or even increasing U.S. aid to many other countries with an abominable human rights record (Thailand, Indonesia, the Philippines, South Korea, El Salvador).

As early as 1977, the State Department noted that national security considerations prevailed even in the case of "small countries whose individual importance for our security may not be great, but whose collective importance may be."[19] As time went on, therefore, human rights was accorded less and less attention as the "national security" mantle was extended to more and more repressive governments. The Administration thus began to campaign for the elimination of restraints on arms transfers to several countries—including Argentina, Guatemala, and Brazil—that had previously been cited for gross human rights violations and were not normally considered vital to U.S. national security.

When Mr. Reagan entered the White House, therefore, **15**

he found that the repressive pipeline was nearly as active as in the Nixon era, and remained fully primed for a major increase in U.S. shipments to dictators abroad. That Mr. Reagan will sanction such increases is without question; all that remains to be seen is the magnitude of these increases and the tack he will take in eliminating the few remaining restraints on repression exports.

In the following four chapters, we will examine the various programs that keep the repression pipeline supplied and functioning. Then, in the Conclusion, we will present some recommendations for curbing repression exports to authoritarian regimes abroad, and show how President Reagan's plans to aid such regimes will ultimately damage U.S. interests.

II:

ARMING THE POLICE:

• THE PUBLIC SAFETY PROGRAM
• INTERNATIONAL NARCOTICS CONTROL

Although most U.S. security assistance programs have been designed to strengthen foreign *military* forces, a major effort has also been made to strengthen the *police* forces of selected pro-U.S. governments. Under the Public Safety program and the International Narcotics Control (INC) program, Washington provided $600 million worth of arms and training to Third World police departments between 1961 and 1980. This amount may not seem very large when compared to the tens of billions provided by the Military Assistance and Foreign Military Sales programs, but because police weapons are less costly than conventional arms (a police revolver, for instance, may cost $250, while a supersonic jet can cost $25 million or more), this sum represents a significant investment in the repressive capabilities of recipient governments. And, as the accompanying tables demonstrate, most of this investment was concentrated in a handful of countries with a particularly poor record on human rights.

The United States first became involved in the supply of repressive technology to Third World police departments in the early 1960s, when counterinsurgency was the principal focus of U.S. strategy. Believing that the police constituted the "first line of defense" against insurgency, U.S. strategists urged President John F. Kennedy to supplement military aid funds with direct assistance to civil security forces. The result was the formation, in 1962, of the Office of Public Safety (OPS). For the next twelve years, OPS provided training to an estimated one million foreign policemen, and funneled some $325 million worth of arms and riot gear to selected Third World regimes.[1] (See Table II.)

The strengthening of Third World police forces appeared a natural goal to U.S. counterinsurgency theorists for a number of reasons. To begin with, the police are regularly interspersed among the population and thus especially well-placed to detect and neutralize anti-government organizations while they are still small and vulnerable. This capability was considered particularly critical in urban areas, where conventional anti-guerrilla techniques were not always applicable and where large concentrations of workers, students, and unemployed *pobladores* (people of the barrios) provided a steady supply of recruits for dissident groups. As former AID Administrator David Bell explained in 1965, "The police are a most sensitive point of contact between government and people, close to the focal points of unrest, and . . . better trained and equipped than the military to deal with minor forms of violence, conspiracy and subversion."[2]

The police were also favored for urban counterinsurgency because they could employ violence *selectively*, against individual dissidents, while the military tended to use force indiscriminately, against whole communities or neighborhoods, thus alienating the population at large. "I think we have to face a reality," Prof. David Burks of Indiana University told the Senate Foreign Relations Committee in 1969. "The reality is that when the insurgents appear, the governments will call upon the Army to eliminate the insurgents . . . But [despite some initial success] there comes a point . . . when the army cannot handle this kind of situation simply because the military establishment tends to use too much force, tends to use the wrong techniques and tends, therefore, to polarize the population and gradually force the majority of those who are politically active to support the revolutionary or insurgent force." The police, on the other hand, are "well integrated with the population" and thus, using selective force, "can often control a crisis before it can escalate into dangerous proportions."[3]

This view gained more and more support as the war in

Vietnam progressed and it became obvious that the large

U.S. military effort was generating more opposition than it ever succeeded in eliminating. "The outstanding lesson [of the Indochina War]," General Maxwell D. Taylor noted at the time, "is that we should never let another Vietnam-type situation arise again. We were too late in recognizing the extent of the subversive threat. We appreciate now that every young, emerging country must be constantly on the alert, watching for those symptoms which, if allowed to develop unrestrained, may eventually grow into a disastrous situation such as that in South Vientam." As a result of this experience, he added, "We have learned the need for a strong police force and a strong police intelligence organization to assist in identifying early the symptoms of an incipient subversive situation."[4]

Out of this analysis evolved the "preventive medicine" doctrine, first articulated by Under Secretary of State U. Alexis Johnson in 1971. By detecting and suppressing dissident organizations in their early stages of development, he explained, the police can prevent the outbreak of full-scale insurgency and thus preclude the need for military intervention. In Johnson's words, "Effective policing is like 'preventive medicine.' The police can deal with threats to internal order in their formative states. Should they not be prepared to do this, 'major surgery' may be required in the sense that considerable force would be needed to redress these threats. This action is painful and expensive and often disruptive in itself."[5]

On the basis of this doctrine, Washington provided steadily increasing subsidies to selected Third World police forces in the late 1960s and early 1970s. Although U.S. officials stressed that such aid was designed to improve overall police capabilities, AID documents indicate that OPS subsidies were not awarded for general law enforcement support but rather given to those particular police agencies deemed most useful to the "preventive medicine" model: intelligence and surveillance units, the "special branch" or political police, riot squads, and paramilitary commando units or "S.W.A.T." (Special Weapons and Tactics) teams. Thus OPS worked with such organizations as SAVAK (the notorious secret police) in

TABLE II
U.S. Assistance to Foreign Police Forces Under the Public Safety Program, Fiscal Years 1961-73
(Current U.S. dollars, in thousands)

Region & Country	Total Expenditures[1]	Students Trained in the U.S.[1]	U.S. Public Safety Advisers[2]
LATIN AMERICA			
Argentina	120	78	—
Bolivia	2,325	64	2
Brazil	8,612	570	1
Chile	2,386	163	—
Colombia	6,944	448	5
Costa Rica	1,921	160	4
Dominican Republic	4,193	204	3
Ecuador	3,915	160	3
El Salvador	2,092	168	1
Guatemala	4,855	377	7
Guyana	1,299	53	—
Honduras	1,741	105	3
Jamaica	780	92	1
Mexico	745	34	—
Nicaragua	315	81	2
Panama	2,148	202	3
Paraguay	—	23	—
Peru	4,142	110	—
Uruguay	2,209	173	4
Venezuela	3,625	541	4
Other/Regional	2,239	36	—
TOTAL	56,606	3,842	43
NEAR EAST & SOUTH ASIA			
Egypt (U.A.R.)	312	99	—
Greece	129	18	—
Iran	1,712	179	—
Jordan	2,536	73	—
Lebanon	149	6	—
Pakistan	8,553	116	1
Saudi Arabia	—	126	7
Turkey	200	24	—
Other/Regional	423	74	—
TOTAL	14,014	715	8

Region & Country	Total Expenditures[1]	Students Trained in the U.S.[1]	U.S. Public Safety Advisers[2]
EAST ASIA			
Burma	195	—	—
Cambodia	2,583	5	—
Indonesia	10,121	146	—
Laos	5,029	82	9
Philippines	5,636	256	8
South Korea	7,432	50	—
South Vietnam	100,809	414	196
Thailand	92,667	607	39
Other/Regional	—	78	—
TOTAL	224,472	1,638	252
AFRICA			
Central African Republic	241	21	—
Chad	527	16	—
Dahomey	323	25	—
Ethiopia	2,924	101	—
Ghana	239	70	2
Ivory Coast	743	7	—
Kenya	697	18	—
Liberia	3,651	120	3
Libya	444	12	—
Malagasy Republic	454	13	—
Niger	398	20	—
Nigeria	3,400	56	—
Somali Republic	4,560	113	—
Tunisia	924	128	1
Zaire	5,417	161	10
Other/Regional	2,043	248	—
TOTAL	26,985	1,129	16
EUROPE, Total	—	38	16
Non-Regional	2,025	—	—
TOTAL	324,102	7,362	319

1. Source: U.S. Agency for International Development, *USAID Operations Report*, data as of June 30, 1973 (Washington, 1973), and earlier editions. 2. Source: U.S. House of Representatives, Committee on Appropriations, *Foreign Assistance Appropriations for FY 1973*. Hearings, 1972, Pt. II, p. 805.

Iran, the paramilitary Carabineros of Chile, ORDEN (a paramilitary spy network) in El Salvador, and the assassination squads of South Vietnam's National Police Force. And because these agencies are directly responsible for the suppression of dissent, OPS support inevitably led to direct and indirect U.S. involvement in widespread abuses of individual human rights. When such involvement finally became too conspicuous to hide or deny, the Public Safety program was abolished—but not before many of its basic functions were transferred, as we shall see, to AID's International Narcotics Control program.

OPS AND THE 'PUBLIC SAFETY' PROGRAM

The United States first supported Third World police forces in 1955, when President Eisenhower agreed to set up "Public Safety Missions" in four countries as part of an effort to shore up pro-U.S. regimes abroad. Although similar advisory groups were later dispatched to a handful of other countries, total spending under the incipient Public Safety Program remained modest throughout the Eisenhower period. In 1962, however, President Kennedy ordered a substantial increase in such assistance as part of the overall expansion of America's counterinsurgency capabilities. Spending was doubled, and the Office of Public Safety was established in the Agency for International Development to coordinate the expanded program. OPS ultimately had a staff of over 400 "Public Safety Advisers" stationed in some 45 foreign countries and a yearly budget of over $50 million.[6]

The Public Safety Program's ostensible aim was to aid in the development of modern, "professional" police forces dedicated to "maintenance of an atmosphere of law and order under humane, civil concepts and control." In practice, this meant the strengthening of the counterinsurgency and social-control capabilities of the police at the expense of all other considerations. OPS officials indicated in 1970 that future Public Safety grants would be used to help security forces of underdeveloped countries enhance their capacity for detecting and "neutralizing" underground organizations, and for "controlling militant activities ranging from demonstrations, disorders, riots through small-scale guerrilla operations."[7]

The Office of Public Safety aided foreign police agencies in three ways:

(1) by making direct grants of police hardware (revolvers, shotguns, rifles, tear-gas grenades, riot sticks, helmets, patrol cars, communications gear, computers, etc.);

(2) by providing advanced training to foreign police officials at the International Police Academy (IPA) in Washington and at other special schools in the United States;

(3) by sending "Public Safety Advisers" to foreign police headquarters to provide training, advice, and technical support.

By the time the Public Safety Program was disbanded in 1975, OPS had distributed some $200 million worth of arms and equipment to foreign police organizations, had trained over 7,500 senior officers at IPA and other U.S. schools, and had provided basic training to over one million rank-and-file policemen at academies abroad (see Table II). In addition, OPS provided technical training to hundreds of foreign police specialists in such subjects as prison design and management (at Southern Illinois University); police records management (at the FBI Academy and the International Police Services School in Washington); maritime law enforcement (at the Coast Guard Academy); and in the design and manufacture of homemade bombs and assassination devices (at a CIA-staffed school at the Border Patrol Academy in Los Fresnos, Texas).*[8]

---

*This final program was officially known as the "Technical Investigations Course." According to OPS documents acquired by Senator James Abourezk in October 1973, the course included lectures and demonstrations on such topics as: Introduction to Bombs and Explosives; Incendiaries; and Assassination Weapons. Ostensibly this course was designed to aid foreign police forces in protecting VIP's against terrorist attacks, but the training was so technical that it could just as easily be used by the police for terrorist attacks of their own. (Indeed, the Defense Department considered the subject matter so inherently

With $50 million to spend annually, OPS obviously could not compete with the much larger Military Assistance Program in arms deliveries. Nevertheless, by concentrating its efforts on the development of key systems—communications, management, training, intelligence, and riot-control—OPS was able to construct modern police infrastructures responsive to Washington's strategic objectives. Thus a 1971 description of the OPS effort in East Asia notes that the Public Safety Program:

> . . . will focus on the development of key institutional elements, such as communciations networks and training systems; on better administration and management leading to the effective use of resources; the improvement of rural paramilitary police ability to prevent and deal with guerrilla activities; the provision of effective police services at the hamlet level; the improvement of urban policing, including the humane [sic] control of civil disturbances and riots.[10]

Similarly, in Latin America, OPS funds were used to: install a centralized "war room" for the Caracas police department; build a unified telecommunications system for Colombia's police and intelligence services; establish the National Police Telecommunications Center and National Institutes of Criminalistics and Identification in Brazil; install a radio teletype network linking the security agencies of five Central American countries; and create an autonomous riot force, the "Cascos Blancos" (White Helmets), in Santo Domingo. These institutions, and similar installatiohs elsewhere, have survived the demise of OPS and constitute a continuing U.S. contribution to repression abroad.

While OPS programs were primarily designed to facilitate the development of institutional resources, the exigencies of the Vietnam war and the Nixon Doctrine forced Washington to play an ever greater role in the

sensitive that it refused to provide instructors for the course.) At least 196 foreign police officers attended this "bomb school" between 1969 and 1973 including many with a long history of human rights violations.[9]

management of internal security operations. Surely the most conspicuous—and most repugnant—product of this effort was the "Operation Phoenix" assassination program in South Vietnam.

The Phoenix program resulted from Washington's belated recognition that Vietnam was primarily a political struggle, and that purely military measures would not produce victory so long as the National Liberation Front continued to "out-govern" the Saigon regime. In essence, Phoenix was a political "search and destroy" operation designed to isolate the NLF's underground administrative apparatus and to "neutralize" (assassinate, imprison, or compromise) its leaders. Although most of the dirty work was performed by indigenous operatives, Phoenix was designed, organized, financed, and administered by U.S. authorities. Inevitably, what started as a wartime measure turned into a massive terror campaign involving U.S. agencies in the wholesale murder, torture, and confinement of the Saigon regime's political opposition.[11]

According to a 1971 statement of former CIA Director William E. Colby, "The Phoenix program includes an intelligence program to identify the members of the VCI [Viet-Cong Infrastructure; i.e., the administrative apparatus of the National Liberation Front], an operational program to apprehend them, a legal program to restrain them, and a detention program to confine them."[12] A somewhat more revealing picture was provided by Wayne Cooper, a former Phoenix adviser in the Mekong Delta, who wrote that Phoenix was a "unilateral American program," wherein CIA operatives "recruited, organized, supplied, and directly paid CT [counter-terror] teams . . . to use Viet Cong techniques of terror—assassinations, ambushes, kidnappings, and intimidation—against the VC leadership."[13] In the years 1968-72 while Phoenix was under direct U.S. administration, a total of 26,369 South Vietnamese civilians were assassinated under the Phoenix program, and another 33,358 were imprisoned under hellish conditions.[14] Some of those "neutralized" (to use Colby's term) through Phoenix must have been actual VCI cadre; the majority, according to the uncontradicted statements of Cooper, were noncommunist nationalists "who expressed fatigue for the war, scorn for Thieu and

Ky, and enthusiasm for a coalition government."[15]

Although Phoenix was primarily a CIA operation, OPS funds were used to underwrite South Vietnamese police participation in the program and to cover some of the "overhead" expenses, such as the construction of additional prison facilities to house the VCI prisoners. Many U.S. officials have testified that torture was a standard part of the Phoenix routine, and an everyday occurrence in the OPS-financed prison facilities. Ultimately it became impossible to disassociate the Public Safety Program from the mounting tide of terror and brutality, and on December 19, 1973, Congress voted to discontinue funding for the South Vietnamese police and prison system.

After Vietnam, the next biggest OPS field operation was mounted in Thailand, where CIA operatives helped establish the Communist Suppression Operations Command (CSOC) to coordinate counterinsurgency operations. Working through CSOC, the Public Safety mission established close relations with all Thai police units, and particularly the Border Patrol Police (BPP), a tough paramilitary force deployed in troubled frontier regions. OPS funds were also used to build 1,000 "tambol" (village) police stations in rural areas, to create a Police Aviation Division with 75 planes and helicopters, and to equip fifty "Special Action" police units modeled on our Special Forces.[16] In addition to conventional police gear, these units received some 2,583 grenade launchers, 74,760 fragmentation grenades, 22,894 mortar shells, and similar ordnance under the Public Safety Program between 1965 and 1972.[17] These arms were used by the BPP in attacks on rebel strongholds in rural areas and in the 1976 assault on Thammasat University in Bangkok. (Although the Public Safety Program was terminated in 1975, Thai police units continue to receive arms and equipment under the International Narcotics Control Program as described below.)

Similar, if less elaborate, programs have been mounted in other Third World areas. Indeed, the CIA has always been closely associated with the Public Safety Program, and in 1974 Colby acknowledged, in a letter to Senator J.

26   William Fulbright, that the Agency worked with OPS "for

the purpose of obtaining foreign intelligence information from cooperative foreign security and intelligence services."[18] That such collaboration went beyond the mere collection of intelligence information is evident from Congressional studies of police operations in Brazil, Guatemala, and the Dominican Republic, where U.S.-equipped units have engaged in periodic roundups of leftist political leaders. In many cases, these sweeps have been accompanied by the torture, assassination, or psychological abuse of prisoners.* Although little "hard" evidence of direct U.S. involvement in these crimes has been produced, a Senate investigating team concluded in 1971 that OPS ties with local security forces were so great that inevitably the United States had become "politically identified with police terrorism" in those countries.[20]

Ultimately, it became impossible to disguise the fundamentally repressive nature of the Public Safety Program. In response to an appeal by Senator Abourezk that the United States cease making "repressive regimes even more repressive,"[21] Congress voted in December 1973 to begin dismantling the Public Safety apparatus. Under the Foreign Assistance Act of 1973, OPS was prohibited from entering into any new police training programs abroad, and a year later—following additional disclosures of OPS abuses—Congress voted to abolish the Public Safety Program altogether. On July 1, 1975, when Section 660 of the Foreign Assistance Act of 1974 took effect, it became illegal to use aid funds, "to provide training or advice, or provide any financial support, for police, prisons, or other law enforcement forces for any foreign government. . . . "

---

*Some of the worst abuses, especially in Latin America, have been attributed to rightist paramilitary "death squads." Often, however, the death squads work in close collaboration with regular security forces, and are themselves composed of off-duty police. A 1981 report by Amnesty International on Guatemala, for example, stated that while the Guatemalan government attributes political killings to independent groups outside its control, detailed evidence shows that they are carried out by the army and police."No convincing evidence has been produced that the groups described by the authorities do in fact exist."[19]

INTERNATIONAL
NARCOTICS CONTROL

Despite passage of Section 660, the dissolution of OPS has not resulted in the termination of U.S. support for foreign police forces. Through the State Department's International Narcotics Control Program (INC) and the Justice Department's Drug Enforcement Administration (DEA), Washington continues to provide equipment, training, and advisory support to many of the same police units it previously aided through OPS. While anti-drug support is ostensibly limited to special narcotics units with drug-control responsibilities, there is ample evidence that INC and DEA programs have simply replaced OPS, thereby contributing to a wide range of politically-motivated internal security and intelligence operations in countries receiving assistance.

In 1971, President Nixon launched a major effort to curb the flow of narcotics into the United States. Part of that effort, headed by a Senior Adviser to the President for International Narcotics Matters, aimed at eliminating foreign sources of supply through U.S.-financed "crop-substitution" programs. At the same time, however, a vast federal bureaucracy was developed to train and advise foreign police officials in narcotics-related work, and to participate directly in anti-drug operations abroad.

The Bureau of International Narcotics Matters in the State Department coordinates the work of numerous federal agencies involved in drug programs abroad. With funds from the International Narcotics Control program, the State Department funds training of foreign police officers by the Drug Enforcement Administration and the U.S. Customs Service. While the Customs Service's anti-drug activities are limited to the training of foreign personnel in border control operations, DEA's mandate extends considerably beyond; in addition to training foreign officers with investigative responsibilities, DEA gathers intelligence on narcotics supply and distribution networks. In this area, it cooperates closely with the CIA (as had OPS before it).[22]

Whatever the differences in intention, the INC-funded programs closely resembled OPS in implementation. Just as in the Public Safety Program, INC programs aid foreign police forces by:

(1) providing grants of arms and equipment designed for police and intelligence activities;

(2) training foreign police officials in the United States and abroad;

(3) assigning U.S. instructors and advisers to foreign police departments.

The evolution of the INC program itself suggests its links to the Office of Public Safety. Until 1971, OPS managed U.S. narcotics programs overseas, and OPS's umbrella organization, the Agency for International Development, continued to implement drug programs abroad after the creation of the Office for International Narcotics Matters. Furthermore, in 1974—the year after Congress voted to terminate the OPS—funding for anti-drug programs jumped over 600%. By 1978, all of INC's personnel in Latin America were former Public Safety advisers brought in from OPS posts around the world.[23] Noting this continuity between OPS and INC, the Government Accounting Office (GAO) observed in 1976 that "Overseas narcotics advisers perform essentially the same functions that public safety advisers used to perform."[24]

Between Fiscal Year 1973 and Fiscal Year 1981, the INC awarded $240 million to law enforcement agencies abroad. Initially, large grants went to countries which had also been major recipients of Public Safety assistance: Argentina, Bolivia, the Philippines, Pakistan, and Thailand. Since Fiscal Year 1979, and after several expressions of Congressional skepticism over the use of these funds, INC allocations have been channeled to those countries considered major sources of drugs entering the United States.* Thus, in Fiscal Year 1980, over 90

*According to estimates by the Drug Enforcement Administration, 65 percent of the heroin entering the United States comes from Mexico, with the remainder coming from the "Golden Triangle" countries of Burma, Thailand, and Laos; most cocaine originates in Bolivia and Peru, with Colombia, Mexico and Ecuador serving as processing and transshipment points; Colombia and Mexico are also the major foreign sources of marijuana.[25]

percent of INC funds went to Mexico, Bolivia, Colombia, Peru, Ecuador, Thailand, Burma, and related regional programs. (See Table III.)

As had OPS, the narcotics program stresses the development of infrastructural elements: training, communications, intelligence, surveillance, and mobility. In the Andean region, for example, INC sponsored a multimillion dollar anti-cocaine "interdiction program" involving the "provision of aerial surveillance equipment, development of rapid mobility capabilities, improvements in domestic and regional communications for the producing, transit and processing countries, and the use of modern [surveillance] equipment to detect and monitor illegal trafficking."[26] In Asia, INC has supplied Burma with 26 helicopters and 5 fixed-wing patrol planes, and has given Thailand 56 sedans, 16 mini-vans, 110 motorcycles, and a wide variety of surveillance devices.[27]

Until Congress specifically outlawed such aid in 1978, the INC program also provided foreign police forces with significant quantities of small arms and riot control equipment, just as OPS had done. Between FY 1973 and FY 1978, for example, INC grants to the Bolivian narcotics enforcement unit included 99 revolvers, and assorted carbines, shotguns, submachine guns, and anti-riot munitions. At the same time, the Ecuadoran National Civil Police and Customs units received 500 carbines, 231 revolvers, and 38 shotguns.[28] These deliveries were usually buried in obscure INC reports, but when publicized by the GAO in 1978,[29] Congress amended Section 481 of the Foreign Assistance Act to prohibit the provision of arms through INC-funded programs.

INC has gone well beyond earlier police programs, moreover, in developing the intelligence-gathering and sharing capabilities of Third World governments. In Latin America, for example, INC funded the establishment of a regional computer network using rented satellite circuits that "ties together Colombia, Peru, Bolivia, Ecuador . . . and the [regional] INTERPOL headquarters in Argentina." According to the INC, "the system will allow each of the countries to communicate directly with the others and through the regional station in Buenos Aires to international [INTERPOL] headquar-

TABLE III:
U.S. Assistance to Foreign Police Forces Under the International Narcotics Control Program, Fiscal Years 1973-81[1]
(Current U.S. dollars, in thousands)

Region & Country	FY73-39	FY80 (planned)	FY81 (proposed)	TOTAL 73-81
LATIN AMERICA				
Argentina	451			451
Bolivia	9,841	2,640	3,300	15,781
Brazil	770			770
Chile	136			136
Colombia	14,498	16,000	3,670	34,168
Costa Rica	118			118
Ecuador	3,116	440	355	3,911
Mexico	76,940	9,410	8,780	95,130
Paraguay	89			89
Peru	3,625	1,720	3,025	8,370
Regional	2,668	640	450	3,758
TOTAL	112,252	30,850	19,580	162,682
NEAR EAST & SOUTH ASIA				
Afghanistan	324			324
Pakistan	2,254	460		2,714
Turkey	5,000			5,000
Regional	197	100	500	797
TOTAL	7,775	560	500	8,835
EAST ASIA				
Burma	32,527	4,600	4,600	41,727
Indonesia	221			221
Laos	4,585			4,585
Philippines	1,008			1,008
Thailand	15,547	2,483	2,740	20,770
Regional	602	285	600	1,487
TOTAL	53,644	7,368	7,940	86,952
ALL COUNTRIES TOTAL	173,674	38,778	28,020	240,272
INTERNATIONAL ORGANIZATIONS	24,853	3,150	3,150	31,153
GRAND TOTAL	198,527	41,928	31,170	271,625

1. Source: U.S. Department of State, *International Narcotics Control*, Fiscal Year 1981 Budget, Congressional Submission (Washington, D.C., 1980), and earlier editions.

ters in Paris."[30] INC funds have also been used in Thailand, Bolivia, and Mexico to create computerized narcotics intelligence data systems to improve "in-country intelligence collection and dissemination."[31] Although there is as yet no direct evidence of the use of INC-funded computer networks for non-drug operations, it is known that certain recipient regimes have used computer technology to trade information on political dissidents. (See Chapter V.)

Theoretically, equipment provided under INC programs can only be supplied to professional anti-drug units. However, a 1976 GAO report to Congress revealed that some foreign governments had arbitrarily labelled regular police units as narcotics squads in order to qualify for INC grants. Many of the infrastructural systems provided by INC, moreover, consist of "common use facilities" that can be used by political police just as readily as by narcotics squads. In Thailand, for example, the GAO found that "commodities supplied [under INC] are basically the same as those furnished under the Public Safety program and go to the same Thai National Police Department elements that had received Public Safety support."[32]

To compound the problem, managers of the INC programs overseas have not developed effective "end-use monitoring" systems to insure that equipment transferred to narcotics units is not diverted for other purposes. A 1978 report by AID's Auditor General revealed, for example, that vehicles provided to Paraguay were being used by the Ministry of the Interior, which has jurisdiction over police "internal security" activities. In Bolivia, GAO investigators could not track INC-provided revolvers, carbines, and submachine guns. In 1978, the GAO observed that "formal end-use monitoring systems had not been established in Bolivia or Peru," and that "although such a system had been established in Colombia, program managers did not believe it was adequate to ensure that equipment was not being diverted [to non-drug programs]."[33]

In addition to providing equipment and logistical support, INC also funds the training provided by DEA and Customs to foreign police officials. Both agencies

32

bring high- and middle-level foreign officials to the United States for "executive seminars" and "mid-management" courses, and send "mobile training teams" overseas to provide training at "in-country" schools for rank-and-file narcotics officers.

Between 1969 and 1978, DEA trained 11,815 foreign police officials at the Advanced International Drug Enforcement School in Washington, D.C., at various in-country schools, and through special executive observation programs which bring foreign officials to tour U.S. facilities. Customs trained 5,111 foreign officers at the U.S. Customs Academy, and at in-country seminars around the globe. (See Table IV.)

While many of the course offerings—pharmacology, drug identification, narcotics treaties—have a clear application to international drug enforcement, a substantial number have much wider political implications. The program of instruction for both DEA's Advanced International School and for the International Drug Enforcement Mobile Schools includes courses in surveillance, undercover operations, raid planning, interview and interrogation, arrest techniques, and the use and development of informants. Courses offered by Customs include verification of declarations and entry documents, personal search, interview and interrogation, communications and intelligence, search of vehicles, and port and border surveillance methods.[34]

As in the case of equipment grants by INC, U.S. officials cannot be sure that training provided for narcotics control is not used for other purposes. According to the GAO, "DEA, Customs, and the Department of State had not systematically evaluated whether U.S.-trained officials were being used in narcotics work ... for the most part [they] did not know what former participants were doing."[35] That such training is used by its recipients for purposes other than narcotics control is supported by U.S. government statistics, and by the practices of the recipients themselves. According to INC's own figures, only 63 percent of foreign police officials trained by the United States remained in narcotics-related work. (These figures cover Fiscal 1976-78 only, and do not include all countries which receive INC funds.) In certain countries, the

TABLE IV:
Training of Foreign Police Personnel by the Drug Enforcement Administration and the U.S. Customs Service, Fiscal Years 1969-78[1]

Region & Country	Drug Enforcement Administration			U.S. Customs Service		
	U.S.	Abroad	Total	U.S.	Abroad	Total
LATIN AMERICA						
Antigua	—	—	—	5	26	31
Argentina	27	526	553	49	107	156
Aruba	—	8	8	7	—	7
Bahamas	11	38	49	2	20	22
Barbados	7	55	62	15	191	206
Bolivia	38	357	395	18	100	118
Brazil	57	516	573	—	51	51
Chile	37	273	310	—	—	—
Colombia	48	525	573	18	336	354
Costa Rica	13	88	101	5	5	10
Dominica	—	—	—	1	—	1
Dominican Rep.	10	76	86	—	40	40
Ecuador	40	198	238	31	195	226
El Salvador	3	11	14	—	5	5
Grenada	—	—	—	2	—	2
Guatemala	19	145	164	—	10	10
Haiti	4	6	10	—	—	—
Honduras	4	9	13	2	5	7
Jamaica	14	124	138	6	56	62
Mexico	31	556	587	5	108	113
Neth. Antilles	11	64	75	12	124	136
Nicaragua	2	10	12	—	5	5
Panama	25	244	269	9	187	196
Paraguay	11	80	91	—	30	30
Peru	61	405	466	12	130	142
St. Lucia	2	3	5	—	—	—

Country						
St. Martin	—	2	2	—	—	—
St. Vincent	—	2	2	—	—	—
Surinam	1	5	6	3	—	3
Trinidad & Tobago	1	64	65	—	—	—
Turks & Caicos Is.	—	1	1	—	—	—
Uruguay	14	134	148	6	181	187
Venezuela	35	340	375	10	119	129
TOTAL	526	4865	5391	218	2031	2249

NEAR EAST & SOUTH ASIA

Country						
Abu Dhabi (United Arab Emirates)	2	—	2	9	38	47
Afghanistan	9	42	51	4	—	4
Bahrain	2	2	4	2	—	2
Egypt	19	117	136	11	113	124
Guam	—	—	—	—	52	52
India	1	—	1	2	—	2
Iran	26	120	146	6	154	160
Israel	1	32	33	1	146	147
Jordan	8	108	116	14	120	134
Kuwait	2	—	2	—	—	—
Lebanon	13	60	73	10	85	95
Nepal	9	1	10	7	85	92
Pakistan	8	206	214	1	110	111
Papua New Guinea	—	—	—	1	44	45
Qatar	2	—	2	2	—	2
Saudi Arabia	2	1	3	10	—	10
Sri Lanka	—	—	—	4	—	4
Syria	—	3	3	7	—	7
Tahiti	1	—	1	—	—	—
Turkey	26	310	336	7	80	87
TOTAL	131	1002	1133	98	1027	1125

Region & Country	Drug Enforcement Administration			U.S. Customs Service		
	U.S.	Abroad	Total	U.S.	Abroad	Total
AFRICA						
Algeria	1	1	2	1	25	26
Ethiopia	—	50	50	5	—	5
Ghana	—	—	—	4	—	4
Liberia	—	—	—	2	29	31
Libya	2	—	2	—	—	—
Malta	—	61	61	—	—	—
Morocco	11	153	164	6	126	132
Nigeria	—	—	—	3	—	3
South Africa	—	180	180	—	—	—
Tunisia	9	78	87	6	41	47
TOTAL	23	523	546	27	221	248
SOUTHEAST ASIA						
Burma	7	—	7	4	—	4
Cambodia	2	—	2	2	—	2
Hong Kong	8	8	16	3	—	3
Indonesia	20	127	147	8	130	138
Laos	14	—	14	13	50	63
Malaysia	14	107	121	9	236	245
Philippines	43	183	226	12	159	171
Singapore	12	180	192	8	103	111
South Korea	12	207	219	4	102	106
Taiwan	14	60	74	10	132	142
Thailand	77	804	881	19	345	364
Vietnam	3	307	310	27	113	140
TOTAL	226	1983	2209	119	1370	1489
WORLD TOTAL	906	8373	9279	462	4649	5111

1. Source: U.S. Department of Justice, *DEA International Training Statistics*; U.S. Customs Service, *International Narcotics Control Training Programs*; documents received by the authors under the Freedom of Information Act.

percentage was even lower: according to the GAO, of 225 Chilean officers trained by the DEA, only 65, or 29 percent, continued to work in a narcotics unit. Of 382 trained in Peru, only 110, again 29 percent, remained in anti-drug work.*[36]

Furthermore, while the 278 DEA agents stationed in 54 offices abroad are theoretically restricted to narcotics-related efforts, they are obviously in a position to engage in non-drug activities. These operatives are required to provide "intelligence expertise and technical assistance" to local police agencies, a task that can easily serve as a cover—as did OPS—for political operations.[38] That they actually do so is suggested by the fact that, in 1973, the head of DEA's Special Operations Division was a former CIA operative, as were 14 members of his staff of 19. And, of the 322 employees in the DEA Office of Intelligence in 1975, 36 were former CIA agents. The Drug Agency openly admits that its agents work in close collaboration with foreign intelligence agencies and with overseas-based agents of the CIA and FBI. In 1975, moreover, a three-man Justice Department team ordered by then Attorney General Edward Levi to investigate charges of "fraud, irregularity, and misconduct" by the DEA uncovered a DEA plot to assassinate Panamanian General Omar Torrijos.[39]

While much of the evidence suggesting a direct link between anti-drug operations and abuses of civil and

---

*Like other facets of the U.S. anti-drug effort abroad, DEA's training has also had the effect of increasing contact between police and intelligence officials who otherwise cooperate for their own political purposes. DEA's Latin American Criminal Investigations Research School, for example, has brought together officers from Argentina, Chile, Paraguay, Colombia, Ecuador, Panama, Peru, and Venezuela in courses designed to "illustrate how an intelligence unit can support current investigations by bringing together information from all sources." The school provides "an in-depth study of the collection, evaluation, analysis, integration, and interpretation of all available information which concerns one or more aspects of criminal activity which is immediately or potentially significant to police planning."[37] Although there is no hard evidence linking these programs to political repression, it is not too difficult to imagine how such skills could be used by the police of these countries for the surveillance and harassment of political dissidents.

political rights is circumstantial, in several cases there are concrete reasons for suspicions of abuse. In Argentina, for example, former police corporal and Minister of Social Welfare Jose Lopez Rega inaugurated an INC-funded program in 1974 by stating that "guerrillas are the main users of drugs. Therefore, the anti-drug campaign will automatically be an anti-guerrilla campaign as well."[40] (Lopez Rega is reportedly one of the founders of the right-wing death squad, the Argentine Anti-communist Alliance). In several countries, moreover, government and private investigations of overseas narcotics programs have uncovered substantial evidence of corruption, the use of torture, and the use of drug monies for counterinsurgency. Mexico and Burma, two countries specially targeted in U.S. anti-drug efforts, are two such cases which deserve a closer look:

Mexico: In 1975, the State Department, CIA and DEA drafted a Narcotics Control Action Plan for Mexico, calling for a concentrated effort in the northwestern mountainous states of Sinaloa, Durango, and Chihuahua, where an estimated 75% of Mexican poppies and marijuana are grown.*[41] INC oversaw the delivery of what one Mexican official described as the largest fleet of non-military aircraft in Latin America—64 helicopters, 24 airplanes, and sophisticated radar, remote sensing, night vision, and communications equipment.[45]

In 1977 DEA launched Operation CONDOR, an anti-drug effort targeted on the area of eastern Sinaloa province. Some 1,800 Mexican Army troops participated in this INC-

---

*DEA also coordinated Operation TRIZO, a plan for the aerial spraying and eradication of drug-producing plants. In 1977 alone, Mexican troops using U.S. equipment sprayed over 22,000 acres of land in the drug-producing regions.[42] The effect, according to sources in the Catholic Church, was that herbicides sprayed on Indian lands were destroying food crops and "driving the population to hunger."[43] A 1979 report prepared by the MITRE Corporation for INC on the environmental effects of eradication programs in Mexico, moreover, concluded only that "no data are available on herbicidal pollutant levels in streams and groundwater in the spray zone," and that "the effect . . . on non-target crops is not known."[44] MITRE admitted, however, that its investigators examined only the pilots and ground support personnel involved in the spraying program—not the area's civilian and peasant population.

funded venture, while DEA advisers worked with agents of the Mexican Federal Judicial Police in Sinaloa's capital of Culiacan, a major center of the international drug trade.[46] One year later, Mexico's Academy of Lawyers charged that hundreds of peasants suspected of growing opium poppies and marijuana had been tortured under Operation CONDOR; testimony from 457 prisoners at the Sinaloa State Penitentiary confirmed that ninety percent of those interviewed by the College of Lawyers were not major traffickers, but local peasants and youths illegally detained and forced to sign confessions under torture.*[47] Despite the rampant abuses of Operation CONDOR, however, State Department officials continue to tout it as a model program, and in 1979 INC reported that U.S. funds would be used "to establish additional zones in Mexico that will be designed upon the model of the successful effort in Sinaloa."[50]

Burma: If there are grounds to question DEA involvement in Mexico, there must be room for equal suspicion in Burma, another major recipient of INC funds. According to the DEA, as much as one-third of Burmese opium is produced in areas controlled by the Burmese Communist Party or by the insurgent Shan and Kachin tribes.[51] To assist the Burmese Army in controlling the drug traffic, the United States has provided Burma with 26 troop-carrying helicopters, 5 fixed-wing aircraft, communications equipment, and other commodities useful in "spotting the more elusive human caravans"[52] which transport opium to the border.

Investigators from the House Select Committee on

---

*According to research conducted by Craig Pyes of the Center for Investigative Reporting, both the DEA regional Administrator for Mexico and Central America, and the U.S. Embassy in Mexico's drug attache denied charges of human rights abuses under CONDOR. Other high officials in the White House and State Department reportedly were aware of the practices of the Mexican Federal Judicial Police, but maintained that DEA's programs had a "mitigating effect" on such abuses.[48] Agents of the Mexican Federal Judicial Police claim that DEA knew of the tortures and sometimes participated in them. Indeed, *San Diego Union* reporter Alex Drehsler quoted DEA head Peter Bensinger as claiming that "our agents are instructed to leave the room when the torture begins."[49]

Narcotics, however, found a much different picture than that painted by U.S. drug officials when they visited Burma in 1977. According to the investigators, ". . . witnesses from the Shan State provided us with convincing evidence that Burma's antinarcotics campaign is a form of economic warfare aimed at the subjugation of its Minority Peoples. We have received testimony of Shan opium fields harvested by Burmese soldiers for their own profit, of tribal opium fields destroyed without compensation, of helicopter-borne troops burning rice fields and villages in the Kachin areas, and of livestock driven off the Karen area."*[53]

In conclusion, it is obvious that the INC and DEA programs can be used to support non-drug activities in violation of the Foreign Assistance Act. Certainly the abuses discovered in Mexico and Burma, as well as GAO findings regarding the use of INC-funded equipment and training elsewhere, suggest that improprieties are widespread, and may even have been intended as U.S. officials sought to continue anti-dissident programs originally sponsored by the defunct Office of Public Safety. Legislators clearly intended in terminating the OPS program that its activities "should not be transferred to some other agency of the government in order to avoid this prohibition."[55] It is clear, however, that such statements have not, by themselves, been entirely effective. While no one can doubt the importance of measures to combat the international drug trade, it is obviously necessary to adopt stringent controls on DEA and INC-funded programs abroad.

---

*Congressman Lester Wolfe, chairman of the Select Committee, also observed that "It should be kept in mind that the leaders of the major trafficking groups have repeatedly offered to work with the United States to eliminate the cultivation of opium. Our only response has been the provision of helicopters to the Burmese government which as been trying to subdue the minority groups for more than 15 years."[54]

III.

THE PENTAGON CONNECTION:

• THE MILITARY ASSISTANCE PROGRAM
• THE FOREIGN MILITARY SALES PROGRAM

In accordance with the national security doctrine described in Chapter 1, the United States has long provided arms and other assistance to the military forces of friendly governments. Such aid has consisted of direct grants of arms and equipment through the Military Assistance Program (MAP), training of foreign military personnel through the International Military Education and Training Program (IMET), credit-assisted arms sales under the Foreign Military Sales (FMS) credit program, deliveries of "surplus" U.S. arms under the Excess Defense Articles (EDA) program, and cash subsidies or loans to immediately threatened governments from the Economic Support Fund (ESF).* Between 1950 and 1979, the United States provided foreign governments a total of $107.3 billion under these programs (includes $53.7 billion in MAP funds, $1.9 billion in IMET funds, $19.6 billion in FMS credits, $6.4 billion in EDA grants, and $25.4 billion from the ESF), with the largest amounts going to a handful of strategically-located regimes in the Near East, Southeast Asia and the Far East.[1] (See Table V and Appendix.)

In addition, the United States has sold foreign

---

*The ESF program was formerly known as the Security Supporting Assistance program.

TABLE V:
U.S. Military Assistance to Selected Recipients, Fiscal Years 1950-79[1]
(Includes the top ten non-NATO recipients plus Greece and Turkey; current U.S. dollars in millions.)

Country	MAP	FMS Credits	IMET	EDA	ESF/SSA	Total
S. Vietnam	14,773.9	—	302.1	1,100.5	5,378.5	21,555.0
Israel	—	11,104.2	—	—	3,554.5	14,658.7
S. Korea	5,129.4	1,084.4	156.1	667.5	2,332.0	9,369.4
Turkey	3,136.0	785.0	111.4	857.7	873.6	5,763.7
Taiwan	2,554.2	547.7	103.2	941.8	727.4	4,874.3
Egypt	—	1,500.0	0.6	—	3,369.7	4,870.3
Greece	1,681.7	852.5	46.2	451.0	348.9	3,380.3
Laos	1,460.1	—	42.8	97.8	774.0	2,374.7
Thailand	1,158.2	133.9	75.0	243.2	414.8	2,025.1
Kampuchea	1,178.5	—	14.6	85.2	543.3	1,821.6
Jordan	467.6	392.8	9.3	46.0	840.7	1,756.4
Iran	766.7	496.4	67.4	61.6	205.3	1,597.4
Sub-Total	32,306.3	16,896.9	928.7	4,552.3	19,362.7	74,046.9
WORLDWIDE TOTAL	53,717	19,855	1,949	6,374	25,414	107,309

1. Source: U.S. Dept. of Defense, *Foreign Military Sales and Military Assistance Facts* (Washington, D.C.: 1980); and U.S. Agency for International Development, *U.S. Overseas Loans and Grants* (Washington, D.C.: 1980).

governments some $121 billion worth of arms and other military hardware through the FMS cash sales and Commercial Sales programs through Fiscal 1980.[2] Although not strictly "aid" in the sense of MAP and IMET, these sales programs are considered a form of assistance to countries which lack an indigenous arms-making capability, and are thus grouped with other aid programs under the general heading of "Security Assistance."

For the most part, these Security Assistance programs are designed to strengthen the capacity of friendly governments to defend themselves against external attack. As we have seen, however, U.S. national security doctrine has consistently stressed the need to defend pro-U.S. regimes against their domestic enemies, and so these programs have always included provision for the support of "internal security" agencies. Such forces have included both regular military units assigned to an occasional internal security role, as well as to paramilitary and gendarme units such as the Philippines Constabulary and the Imperial Iranian Gendarmerie which have an explicit internal security role. Because units of this type are often used to suppress demonstrations, strikes, and other forms of dissent, and because many of the governments receiving such aid are ruled by military or martial-law regimes, U.S. Security Assistance programs constitute a significant form of support for repression abroad.

In the following pages, we will examine these programs in more detail, and show how they contribute to the repressive capabilities of foreign governments. The first section of this chapter will cover the grant aid programs—MAP, IMET, etc.—while the second section will cover the sales programs.*

---

*In discussing these programs our emphasis will be on showing how U.S. aid contributes *directly* to internal repression; we should always remember, however, that *any* form of assistance to the armed forces of Third World governments can promote the ascendancy of the military over civilian institutions (especially in countries where the military has traditionally played a dominant role in national politics), and thus can represent a form of indirect support for militarism and authoritarianism abroad.

THE MILITARY ASSISTANCE PROGRAM, IMET, AND OTHER GRANT PROGRAMS

In the 1950s, U.S. aid policy stressed the development of conventional military forces, and MAP donations therefore tended to consist of standard combat equipment: tanks, artillery, bombers, etc. But then, following the Cuban Revolution of 1959, counterinsurgency and internal war became the principal focus of U.S. strategists. In the 1960s, and especially as the Vietnam War escalated, MAP grants included large quantities of anti-guerrilla hardware: helicopters, cross-country vehicles, surveillance gear, etc. As then-Secretary of Defense Robert S. McNamara explained in 1967, the MAP program in Latin America "will provide no tanks, artillery, fighter aircraft, or combat ships. The emphasis is on vehicles and helicopters for internal mobility [and] communications equipment for better coordination of in-country security efforts."[3]

For most of the 1960s and early 1970s, counterinsurgency constituted the principal rationale for U.S. military assistance programs. All told, Washington provided $26 billion in MAP grants between 1960 and 1974, with the largest amounts going to South Vietnam, Thailand, and other Third World regimes threatened by guerrilla forces. In many cases, U.S. aid was not limited to arms, but also included training, technical assistance, and in-country advisory support by U.S. counterinsurgency experts. At one time, hundreds of U.S. military advisors actively supported anti-guerrilla campaigns in such countries as Thailand, Laos, and the Philippines. In some of these countries, U.S. assistance enabled government forces to overcome insurgent threats and establish stable—if highly militarized and authoritarian—political systems. (Indeed, it might be said that the U.S. role in the formation and survival of these regimes represents the greatest long-term U.S. contribution to repression in the Third World.) When counterinsurgency programs did not produce the desired stability—as in South Vietnam— Washington elected to employ its own troops in a long and ultimately futile struggle to defeat guerrilla forces.

The U.S. failure in Vietnam did not diminish Washington's commitment to counterinsurgency, but it did force changes in the orientation and structure of the aid programs. As noted in Chapter II, much greater emphasis was placed on the development of police and paramilitary forces that could serve as a "first line of defense" against insurgency. And to reduce the risk of American involvement in future Vietnams, Washington sought to create "surrogate gendarmes" like Iran that could assume responsibility for regional stability in critical areas.

To ensure the success of all these efforts, MAP aid was increased steadily from $2.3 billion in Fiscal 1970 to $4.2 billion in Fiscal 1973. As the war in Vietnam became more unpopular, however, Congress proved increasingly disinclined to approve large MAP appropriations, and began to impose tough restrictions on future aid. Initially, Congress banned assistance to the particular regimes implicated in the Indochina war—Vietnam, Laos, and Cambodia. Then, as MAP aid *itself* became seen as an invitation to more Vietnams—and a drain on the U.S. Treasury at a time of growing economic strains (caused, in part, by the OPEC oil price increase of 1974)—Congress voted to abolish the MAP program altogether, although permitting continued aid to a few favored countries which house U.S. bases or otherwise support U.S. military operations. As a result, MAP appropriations declined from $4.2 billion in Fiscal 1973 to only $265 million in 1976, and have remained at that level ever since (see Table VI).*

In response to these setbacks, U.S. officials have developed several alternative channels for the support of pro-U.S. regimes abroad. To begin with, military *sales*—both for cash and credit—were increased dramatically, from $1 billion per year in the early 1970s to $15 billion annually by the end of the decade. U.S. arms firms were

---

*In its first foreign aid proposal to Congress, however, the Reagan Administration asked for $100 million in MAP funds, to be used at its discretion in international emergencies. The revival of the MAP program, Administration spokesmen said, was needed "to help the Administration response quickly and flexibly to international crises" (see the *New York Times*, March 10, 1981).

TABLE VI:
Foreign Military Sales and Military Assistance Trends, Fiscal Years 1971-80[1]
(Current U.S. dollars in millions)

Worldwide Totals:	1971	1972	1973	1974	1975	1976	1977	1978	1979	1980 est.	Total
FMS Agreements	1,395.1	2,980.6	5,305.1	10,381.2	15,830.6	14,817.8	8,793.6	11,746.4	13,025.5	13,500.0	97,775.9
FMS Credits	741.1	547.6	530.9	2,889.4	848.8	2,784.7	1,911.0	2,101.0	5,673.0	2,090.0	20,117.5
Commercial Sales Deliveries	427.5	480.6	362.1	502.2	546.6	1,402.0	1,523.4	1,676.0	1,389.0	1,980.0	10,289.3
MAP Grants	3,050.5	3,473.1	4,209.0	1,529.2	1,049.8	265.1	245.4	219.1	224.1	145.5	14,410.9

1. Source: U.S. Dept. of Defense, *Foreign Military Sales and Military Assistance Facts* (Washington, D.C.: 1980); and U.S. Dept. of Defense, *Security Assistance Program*, Congressional Presentation Document, F.Y. 1981 (Washington, D.C.: 1980).

also permitted to increase their sales to foreign police and security organizations through State Department and Commerce Department channels (see Chapters 4 and 5). And, in order to preserve the training and advisory elements of the MAP program, these functions were separated out and financed separately under the International Military Education and Training Program (IMET).

Under Section 541 of the Foreign Assistance Act, the Department of Defense is authorized to furnish "military education and training to military and related civilian personnel of foreign countries," under terms and conditions established by the President. Such training is provided at scores of military schools in the United States, and at the U.S. Army School of the Americas (USARSA) in the Panama Canal Zone.* All told, over one-half million foreign military officers and technicians have received some training under the IMET program and its predecessors since 1950. (See Table VII for a country-by-country breakdown of total students trained under IMET; for IMET expenditures by country, see Appendix.)

At $30 million dollars per year, the IMET program hardly compares with the multibillion-dollar scale of the original MAP program. Pentagon officials insist, however, that it represents an extremely worthwhile allocation of U.S. funds because it fosters "military-to-military relationships of enduring value" between American and foreign officers. Such relationships are particularly valuable, according to the Department of Defense, because "many of these trainees now occupy positions from which they are able to influence favorably the receptivity of their armed forces and their governments to U.S. ideals, methods, and standards."[4] In recognition of such interservice links, moreover, former Secretary of Defense

---

*Among the hundreds of institutions which provide training to foreign military personnel are: U.S. Army Infantry School, Ft. Benning, GA; U.S. Army Military Police School, Ft. Gordon, GA; U.S. Army Intelligence School, Ft. Huachuca, AZ; U.S. Army Institute for Military Assistance (the "Green Beret" school), Ft. Bragg, NC; Naval Amphibious School, Coronado, CA; Naval War College, Newport, RI; and Naval Guided Missile School, Dam Neck, VA.

TABLE VII:
Training of Foreign Military Personnel by the United States, Fiscal Years 1950-79[1]

(Students trained under the Military Assistance Program and International Military Education and Training Program)

Country		Country		Country		Country	
Afghanistan	487	France	14,399	Liberia	677	South Korea	34,464
Argentina	4,017	Ghana	332	Libya	567	South Vietnam	47,743
Austria	444	Greece	14,515	Luxembourg	157	Spain	10,788
Bangladesh	56	Guatemala	3,334	Malaysia	739	Sri Lanka	57
Barbados	1	Guinea	4	Mali	70	Sudan	213
Belgium	5,118	Haiti	632	Mexico	964	Syria	20
Benin	16	Honduras	3,445	Morocco	2,660	Taiwan	25,593
Bolivia	4,861	Iceland	30	Nepal	62	Thailand	17,764
Brazil	8,659	India	645	Netherlands	6,506	Togo	4
Burma	878	Indochina	434	Nicaragua	5,673	Tunisia	1,146
Cameroon	6	Indonesia	5,614	Niger	4	Turkey	19,193
Chile	6,883	Iran	11,025	Nigeria	472	United Kingdom	3,970
Colombia	7,907	Iraq	406	Norway	5,501	Upper Volta	25
Costa Rica	696	Italy	9,622	Pakistan	4,891	Uruguay	2,806
Cuba	523	Ivory Coast	50	Panama	4,894	Venezuela	5,540
Denmark	4,657	Jamaica	11	Papua New Guinea	2	West Germany	1,532
Dominican Republic	4,218	Japan	15,681	Paraguay	2,018	Yemen	87
Ecuador	5,958	Jordan	2,051	Peru	7,966	Yugoslavia	843
Egypt	36	Kampuchea	67,464	Philippines	16,363	Zaire	914
El Salvador	1,971	Kenya	121	Portugal	3,643	General, Regional and Other	62
Ethiopia	3,912	Laos	44,497	Saudi Arabia	1,425	WORLDWIDE TOTAL	495,367
Finland	60	Lebanon	1,636	Senegal	37		

1. Source: U.S. Defense Security Assistance Agency, *Foreign Military Sales and Military Assistance Facts* (Washington, D.C.: 1979), pp. 31-2.

McNamara once told a Congressional subcommittee: "Probably the greatest return on our military assistance program investment comes from the training of selected officers and key specialists at our military schools and training centers in the United States and overseas. These students . . . are the coming leaders, the men who will have the know-how and impart it to their forces. I need not dwell upon the value of having in positions of leadership men who have first-hand knowledge of how Americans do things and how they think. *It is beyond price to us to make such friends of such men.*"[5] (Emphasis added.)

Ostensibly, IMET training involves the same technical military subjects—tank maneuvers, infantry operations, amphibious warfare, etc.—that are taught to American trainees. However, in accordance with the internal-security orientation that has always been a part of the overall MAP conception, IMET training also includes instruction in specialized topics of particular relevance to counterinsurgency and anti-dissident operations. Thus the Army's Military Police School at Ft. Gordon, Georgia, has provided training to foreign military personnel in such subjects as: Criminal Investigation, Security Management, Civil Disturbance Orientation, Polygraph ("lie-detector") Examiner, and Military Police Investigator. At the Army School of the Americas, moreover, Latin American trainees have received training in: Counterinsurgency Operations, Urban Counterinsurgency, Military Intelligence Interrogator, and Military Explosives and Detonators (see Table VIII). Although portrayed as conventional military instruction by U.S. officials, these courses appear far more relevant to political warfare and the suppression of dissent.[6] And despite all that was said about human rights during his Administration, President Carter continued to authorize training in these subjects for officers from many repressive countries including Indonesia, Thailand, the Philippines, Morocco, Zaire, Haiti, Paraguay, and El Salvador.*

---

*Indeed, when insurgent forces increased their attacks on the military-civilian *junta* in El Salvador in 1980, Carter approved a crash program in counterinsurgency training to 250 Salvadorean officers at the Army School of the Americas—prompting Panamanian President

At one time, MAP aid and training was provided not only to foreign military officers, but to police and paramilitary officers as well. In 1974, however, the Defense Department agreed to terminate its assistance to civil security forces in line with Section 660 of the Foreign Assistance Act. Nevertheless, Pentagon officials have interpreted this provision to allow continued support for units and facilities which perform civil security missions as part of their regular duties. This interpretation, according to the General Accounting Office, has enabled the Pentagon to support anti-dissident operations in three ways:[8]

(1) *Through rotation of IMET-trained personnel:* Although the Pentagon is legally barred from providing training to foreign police, it regularly trains military officers who at some point in their careers are assigned to police duties. Such "rotation" is customary in many Third World countries, where the armed forces often perform internal security functions in addition to their regular military duties. And while the Pentagon has eliminated conventional police topics from courses given to foreign military personnel, it continues to provide training in closely-related subjects such as military police operations and urban counterinsurgency.

(2) *Through support of dual-purpose units:* The Pentagon interprets the Foreign Assistance Act to bar MAP and IMET aid to military units performing "ongoing" police tasks, but to permit aid when they do so on a "contingency" or irregular basis. Such distinctions are necessarily vague—particularly in countries where the military is engaged in protracted counterinsurgency operations—and it is not surprising that the GAO found that U.S. aid and training is being provided to many paramilitary units which are in fact doing police work, such as the Philippines Constabulary and the Saudi

Aristides Royo to charge that Washington was contributing to internal repression in El Salvador. In an Orwellian attempt to disguise the repressive nature of this program, Administration officials labeled the course "Human Rights Aspects in International Defense and Development" and argued that it would help promote respect for human rights on the part of Salvadorean officers.[7]

TABLE VIII:

Training of Foreign Military Personnel at the U.S. Army School of the Americas, Panama Canal Zone, Fiscal Years 1976-80[1] (Selected courses)

	Command & General Staff	Small Unit Training Management	Communications Chief	Combat Arms Basic	Combat Engineers	Infantry Qualification (Cadet Course) Officer	Infantry Officer Basic	Infantry Officer Advanced	Infantry Tactics & Techniques	Small Unit Infantry Tactics & Techniques	Small Unit Infantry Tactics	Irregular Warfare Operations	Joint Operations	Command Operations	Jungle Operations	Military Explosives	Mortar Training	Patrolling Operations	Internal Security Operations	Military Intelligence
Argentina	10												1		2	6				4
Bolivia	17			391							70		27	3						2
Brazil													3							2
Colombia										252				8				2	228	
Dominican Republic	30						66													
Ecuador	5	2			60	88		3	2			12	1	16	6			46		4
El Salvador	3	5		26				7	2			2	1	18		1				1
Guatemala	3	2						5	6				4							4
Honduras	98	20		72						79		6	8					10		8
Mexico	16												8					8		
Nicaragua	12		1	4		45	9	2	38				4	138	46	6	79			9
Panama	27						6	31	17					40	101	4		110		7
Paraguay	5			2			2	2	1					1					39	
Peru	13							3	6				10	22	57			20	173	4
Uruguay	1																		82	4
Venezuela	23																			3
TOTAL	263	29	30	495	60	133	83	53	72	331	70	20	82	246	212	17	79	196	522	50

1. Source: Tables submitted to the authors by the U.S. Army under the Freedom of Information Act.

Arabian National Guard. This was also the case with Somoza's National Guard in Nicaragua.

(3) *Through aid to countries under martial law:* Many of the countries now receiving MAP aid are governed under martial law or other systems of "emergency" rule. These include South Korea, the Philippines, Thailand, Indonesia, and Morocco. Indeed, in a number of these nations martial law has become a permanent way of life. Typically, the military forces of these countries have been empowered to arrest, detain, investigate, and try civilians suspected of criminal or political offenses, and thus do serve as a civil police. Under the 1974 Foreign Assistance Act, these forces should be barred from receiving arms and training. The GAO found, however, that the Pentagon continues to provide aid in many such cases. Thus the Philippines, long ruled by the martial-law regime of President Marcos, is a major recipient of MAP and IMET assistance.

It should be obvious from all this that the measures adopted by Congress in 1974 to restrict military aid and training to foreign police and security forces have not been successful in cutting off the flow. Statements by Reagan's advisers suggest, moreover, that the new Administration plans substantial increases in U.S. aid to the paramilitary forces of pro-U.S. regimes. (See Chapter 6.)

THE FOREIGN MILITARY SALES PROGRAM

Although *grant* military assistance has dropped significantly since 1973, this decline has been more than offset by an increase in military *sales.* As shown by Table VIII, arms exports under the Foreign Military Sales (FMS) program rose from about $1 billion per year in the early 1970s to nearly $15 billion annually at the end of the decade. Commercial Sales also rose significantly, from $0.5 billion to $1.5 billion. (The FMS program entails sales by the U.S. *Government* from its own arms stocks to foreign governments; Commercial Sales involve exports by U.S. *corporations* to foreign governments, companies, or individuals.) And because most Third World nations lack the wherewithall to buy arms for cash, Washington has steadily increased the amount of *credits* available under the FMS program, from $0.7 billion in 1971 to $5.7 billion in 1979. All told, the United States sold an astounding $93.7 billion worth of arms, ammunition, and related hardware during the 1970s, or eight times the amount sold over the previous twenty years.

As in the case of MAP aid, U.S. sales programs are designed to help friendly governments enhance their self-defense capabilities through deliveries of arms, training, and technical services. Typically, these transactions involve sales of conventional military hardware—tanks, rockets, aircraft, etc.—but, like MAP, also include transfers of counterinsurgency and internal security hardware. Indeed, an examination of Pentagon and State Department documents indicates that the United States is selling Third World governments a wide range of police and paramilitary equipment, including shotguns, tear-gas dispensers, armored cars, helicopters, and light-strike aircraft designed for counterinsurgency missions. Such hardware is exported both through the Pentagon's FMS program and the State Department's Commercial Sales program.* Because FMS sales are handled in much the same way as MAP grants, we will discuss these transactions here, while reserving our discussion of Commercial Sales for Chapter 4.

Under Section 22 of the Arms Export and Control Act (AECA) of 1976, "the President may . . . enter into contracts for the procurement of defense articles or defense services for sale for United States dollars to any foreign country" deemed eligible for such purchases. In these cases, the U.S. Government acts essentially as an arms broker, buying equipment from U.S. producers and then reselling them on a cash or credit basis to foreign governments. Theoretically, such sales are managed by the Department of State, but in practice most FMS

---

*Normally, military-type hardware (helicopters, planes, armored vehicles, machine-guns) are sold through the FMS program while police-type equipment (pistols, revolvers, tear-gas dispensers) are sold through the Commercial Sales program.

transactions are negotiated and consummated by the Pentagon's Defense Security Assistance Agency (DSAA).

Like MAP grants, FMS sales often consist of repression gear used by many Third World governments to engage in continuing struggles with dissident or insurgent movements. Thus an examination of Pentagon data reveals that recent FMS deliveries have included:[9]

To Thailand: 32 Rockwell OV-10 "Bronco" counterinsurgency planes; 20 Fairchild AU-23A "Peacemaker" counterinsurgency planes; 50 Cadillac-Gage V-150 "Commando" armored cars (with 94 more on order).

To the Philippines: 16 Rockwell OV-10 "Bronco" counterinsurgency planes; 20 Cadillac-Gage OV-10 "Commando" armored cars; $169,481 worth of "concertina" barbed wire.

To Malaysia: 400 Cadillac-Gage V-150 "Commando" armored cars.

To Morocco: 6 Rockwell OV-10 "Bronco" counterinsurgency planes; 24 Hughes 500-MD helicopter gunships.

To El Salvador: night vision scopes, M-16 rifles and ammunition, grenade launchers, transport vehicles and sophisticated communications gear.

In addition to providing equipment, the FMS program also supplies training, maintenance, managerial and technological assistance, and other "military technical services" to recipient governments. Such sales now account for 40 percent of all military sales, and, as in the case of hardware sales, involve internal as well as external security functions. In Saudi Arabia, for instance, the Vinnell Corporation is providing training, technical assistance, and advisory support to the Saudi Arabian National Guard—a paramilitary security force—under a $77 million FMS contract. Similarly, in Iran, the Bell Helicopter Company helped establish an Iranian Sky Cavalry Brigade modeled on the U.S. 1st Air Cavalry Division of Vietnam fame. To carry out these projects, U.S. firms often rely on a new breed of mercenaries who sell their technical expertise rather than combat skills. And while these "white collar mercenaries" wear civilian clothes rather than military uniforms, they play key roles in many Third World military establishments and thus represent a *de facto* U.S. military commitment to these governments, including many which have been cited for persistent human rights violations.[10]

Theoretically, FMS sales, like all other "security assistance" programs, are subject to the Section 502(B) ban on transfers to governments which consistently violate human rights. In addition, Congress has imposed restrictions on FMS sales to a few particularly repressive regimes, including Argentina, Chile, and Uruguay; and in 1977, Brazil, Guatemala, and El Salvador joined the list by rejecting U.S. sales credits. Nevertheless, President Carter continued to supply vast quantities of internal security gear to many other governments with an equally dismal record on human rights (e.g., Thailand, the Philippines, Indonesia) and, as the end of his term approached, asked Congress for increases in Foreign Military Sales credits for El Salvador, Honduras, and Morocco for use in controversial counterinsurgency wars. And now, as the Reagan Administration takes over management of the FMS program, it is certain that most remaining human rights restrictions on such sales will be terminated. Reagan's aides have already mentioned Argentina, Brazil and El Salvador as countries which should be fully eligible for FMS deliveries, and it is likely that the new Administration will later move to lift restrictions on other repressive regimes, including Chile and Uruguay.[11] As we move into the 1980s, therefore, it is evident that the FMS program will serve as a major conduit for the supply of repressive technology to authoritarian regimes abroad.

IV.

MERCHANTS OF REPRESSION:

EXPORTS OF POLICE WEAPONS THROUGH THE COMMERCIAL SALES PROGRAM

As noted in Chapter 3, foreign buyers can obtain arms from the United States through two channels: the Foreign Military Sales program and the Commercial Sales (CS) program. FMS sales are negotiated by the U.S. Government and typically involve major weapons systems used by America's own armed forces; Commercial Sales, on the other hand, are negotiated directly by U.S. arms firms and usually involve light weapons and combat-support equipment. Among the items which normally fall into the CS category are police weapons and related equipment (pistols and revolvers, tear-gas grenades, chemical "MACE," armored cars, etc.). Every year, U.S. arms firms sell millions of dollars worth of these weapons to police and paramilitary organizations abroad.

Under the Arms Export and Control Act of 1976 (and predecessor legislation), any firm wishing to export an item on the U.S. Munitions List (a catalog of weapons and "implements of war" classified as military items) through CS channels must first apply for an export license from the Office of Munitions Control (OMC) in the Department of State. Theoretically, these applications are subject to the same human rights standards applied to FMS exports, but in practice, Commercial Sales are often processed with minimal attention. This is partly because most police sales involve relatively small amounts of money (the transactions are not even *reported* to Congress unless they exceed $1 million, a rarity in foreign police orders), and partly because Congress and the Executive Branch have adopted a generally permissive attitude regarding such sales.

The small scale—and relative invisibility—of CS transactions should not allow us to underestimate their contribution to repression abroad. While most sales to foreign police organizations are quite modest—involving perhaps two or three hundred firearms and gas grenades—their collective proportions are quite imposing: according to OMC documents obtained by the authors under the Freedom of Information Act, U.S. arms firms sold Third World police forces a total of 615,612 gas grenades and 126,622 revolvers between September 1976 and May 1979, along with 51,906 rifles, and carbines and submachineguns; 8,870 cannisters of MACE; 3,160 riot guns; and 56 million rounds of ammunition (see Table IX). Recipients of this hardware included police forces in a long list of Third World countries, including many ruled by authoritarian regimes (see Appendix for a complete breakdown of U.S. police exports by country).

CS transactions of this sort have a significant bearing on U.S. human rights policy for several reasons. First of all, they consist of weapons intended *specifically* for civil security purposes. Even under the best of circumstances such deliveries raise fundamental questions of propriety and justice; when sold to undemocratic regimes, however, these weapons automatically become tools of repression. This judgment is even more inescapable when we remember that *these tools are being sold directly to the organizations responsible for the torture, assassination, incarceration, and "disappearance" of political dissidents.* According to the OMC documents obtained by the authors, recipients of such hardware have included SAVAK of Iran (the late Shah's dreaded secret police), the Carabineros of Chile, "Papa Doc" Duvalier's Palace Guard in Haiti, and the Presidential Security Force of South Korea. These weapons have also been sold to the police of Argentina, Brazil, Guatemala, El Salvador, Paraguay, Afghanistan, Iraq, Syria, Indonesia, Singapore, the Philippines, and many other countries noted for their consistent and flagrant abuse of individual human rights.[1] And while the Carter Administration did hold up CS sales to some of the more notorious human rights violators, the overall level of CS sales actually

TABLE IX:
U.S. Arms Sales to Third World Police Forces, September 1976 - May 1979[1]

Region & Country	Gas Grenades & Projectiles	Gas Guns	Cannisters MACE	Rifles, Carbines & Submachine Guns	Pistols & Revolvers	Ammunition (1000 rds.)
LATIN AMERICA						
Antigua	116					26
Bahamas	421					2
Belize	310					34
Bermuda	212	12				
Bolivia				160	310	10
Brazil		100		60	14	5
Cayman Is.					12	
Colombia	48,020	30		395	7,900	250
Costa Rica	150		200			14
Ecuador	11,135	1,000	100		1,853	1,256
El Salvador	852	4			173	
Guatemala	5,000			65	1,006	6,763
Guyana	4,000					
Haiti					20	1
Honduras	1,700				59	418
Jamaica	2,550	32			750	247
Martinique			100		14	
Mexico	2,640	6	1,000	529	1,886	10
Monserrat	200					
Netherlands Antilles	25				54	181
Nicaragua	500			6,054	447	7,312
Panama	1,000			650	243	1,364
Paraguay	48					140
Peru	5,785				17,613	

Region & Country	Gas Grenades & Projectiles	Gas Guns	Cannisters MACE	Rifles, Carbines & Submachine Guns	Pistols & Revolvers	Ammunition (1000 rds.)
St. Kitts	30					
St. Lucia	50					
St. Vincent	50					
Surinam					153	1
Trinidad & Tobago	200		18		7	107
Turks & Caicos Is.	148	2				
Uruguay						100
Venezuela	53,651		205	96	9,088	1,531
Virgin Is.	307	2				
TOTAL:	139,100	1,188	1,623	8,009	41,602	19,772
EAST ASIA & PACIFIC						
Brunei				100		205
Fiji	16					
Hong Kong	21,240	256	1,887		2,050	1,890
Indonesia		64		15,000	1,326	1,367
Macao					554	40
Malaysia	102,629	536	4,140	25,914	16,980	16,029
Papua New Guinea	20		3			10
Singapore	3,528	58			4,234	5,985
S. Korea				374	201	5
Tahiti			25			
Taiwan	4,000		240		7,200	1,372
Thailand	4,315			2,270	702	3,400
TOTAL:	135,748	914	6,295	43,658	33,247	30,303

Region & Country	Gas Grenades & Projectiles	Gas Guns	Cannisters MACE	Rifles, Carbines & Submachine Guns	Pistols & Revolvers	Ammunition (1000 rds.)
AFRICA						
Algeria					1,020	
Botswana	500				13	71
Gambia		4				
Ghana	5,000					
Kenya	300		425			
Lesotho	100					
Liberia		10	175		14,322	203
Malta					100	
Mauritius	300	33				
Morocco		210		100		
Nigeria	88,042					
Senegal					8	
Seychelles					15	10
Swaziland					2	
Tanzania					2	1
Tunisia	12,550	120	50		2,365	40
TOTAL:	106,792	377	650	100	17,847	325
NEAR EAST & SOUTH ASIA						
Abu Dhabi	3,100	3		18	130	140
Afghanistasn					36	10

Region & Country	Gas Grenades & Projectiles	Gas Guns	Cannisters MACE	Rifles, Carbines & Submachine Guns	Pistols & Revolvers	Ammunition (1000 rds.)
Bahrain	6,000	43		6	280	12
Bangladesh	2,300	20				120
Cyprus	900	350			200	328
Egypt	153,946				2,419	
India	17,040				3,060	10
Iran	12,334				420	
Iraq						3,959
Israel	16,557	75	300		166	150
Jordan					3,003	101
Kuwait	200			15		
Lebanon					5,198	70
Nepal	225	14				30
Oman	13,000	160		100	970	49
Pakistan	8,370		2		646	100
Qatar					14,326	330
Saudi Arabia						
Sri Lanka		16			72	25
Syria					3,000	
Turkey						
TOTAL:	233,972	681	302	139	33,926	5,434
WORLD TOTAL	615,612	3,160	8,870	51,906	126,622	55,834

1. Source: Export licenses issued to U.S. arms firms by the Office of Munitions Control, U.S. Department of State.

increased during the Carter years.

Sales of internal security hardware to the police and security forces of authoritarian regimes clearly represent a form of U.S. involvement in repression abroad; in some cases, moreover, that involvement can be explicitly demonstrated:

• During the January 1977 "food riots" in Egypt (a spontaneous protest against price increases for government-subsidized staples which resulted in seventy-five deaths), Robert Fisk of the *London Times* filed this report from Cairo: "One after another, young policemen wearing gas masks ran forward, knelt on one knee and fired cannisters into the crowd . . . Behind them ran three perspiring soldiers carrying dustbins full of replacement gas cartridges. As the crowds noticed with interest, these came not from the country's former military suppliers— the Soviet Union—but from the United States. One group of demonstrators chanted anti-American slogans, charging that all the tear gas came from the United States. Indeed, this appeared to be true. Every empty gas cannister which I picked up bore the words 'CS #518— Federal Laboratories, Inc., Saltsburg, PA.' "[2] (Federal Laboratories is the leading U.S. producer of CS "pepper" gas.)

• Following one of the many student protests against the late Shah of Iran, William Branigin of the *Washington Post* reported from Teheran: "A clash Saturday [November 18, 1978] was the most violent crackdown against dissidents. More than 350 Iranian riot police wearing U.S.-made helmets and armed with wooden truncheons invaded Teheran University and battered students."[3]

• Following a 1978 anti-government demonstration in Sao Paulo, Brazilian journalists reported that several students had been badly burned and/or blinded by a chemical spray fired by government security forces. The spray was reportedly produced by cannisters (some of which were dropped by the police during the melee) which were clearly marked "No. 502 CS Irritant Agent—Federal Laboratories, Saltsburg, PA, USA."[4]

• During the national uprising in Nicaragua in
September, 1978, a reporter from the *Washington Star*

wrote that " . . .grenades were tossed into suspected rebel positions from a C-47 aircraft . . . one soldier was asked about the American M-16 rifles that this country had bought from the Colt Company with a license that specified that they are not to be used in police actions."[5]

These are just a few of the many occasions when U.S. weapons have been used by foreign police forces to suppress dissent over the past few years. No one will ever know how many people were maimed or killed by U.S. weapons in such incidents, but going by the figures for Argentina, Chile, El Salvador, Nicaragua, Iran, Indonesia, and the Philippines (where tens of thousands of civilians have been killed by government forces over the past few years), the total could easily approach the figures for civilian casualties during the Vietnam War.

Despite the clear connection between U.S. police exports and repression abroad, the CS program flourished under President Carter. Indeed, Table X shows a marked increase in arms exports to Third World police forces during the Carter period. And now that Ronald Reagan has occupied the White House, it is likely that such exports will expand at an even faster rate. Because CS deliveries are so directly linked with repression abroad, it is important that we examine this program more closely, and identify the commodities, producers, and exporters involved.

COMMODITIES

Foreign police agencies can purchase almost any item of equipment used by their American counterparts, and even some that are not. Among those in greatest demand abroad, according to the OMC documents, are firearms, gas grenades, and armored cars. A brief description of these products follows:

• **Handguns:** The most popular type is the .38 calibre revolver, of which Smith & Wesson (S&W) and Colt—the leading producers—have sold over 100,000 since 1976. Other popular handguns include .357 and .32 calibre revolvers. The OMC documents indicate that almost every country in the world has acquired at least some U.S. **63**

TABLE X:
U.S. Arms Exports to Third World Police Forces, 1973-76 vs. 1976-79[1]

	1973-76	1976-79	Percent Change[2]
Tear-gas grenades	155,835	615,612	+295
Cannisters of "MACE"	6,633	8,870	+34
Riot guns	5,224	3,160	- 40
Pistols & revolvers	49,936	126,622	+154
Rifles, carbines & submachine guns	9,270	51,906	+460
Rounds of ammunition	7,590,000	55,834,000	+635

1. Source: Export licenses issued by the Office of Munitions Control, U.S. Department of State, to major U.S. arms producers.

2. Note: These figures should be viewed as approximate rather than exact percentages, since there were slight differences in the list of companies involved in the two samples.

handguns, and there are cases where entire police forces have been rearmed. The Royal Malay Police, for instance, bought 16,000 S&W .38's in 1978, and the Peruvian Civil Guard bought 10,000 Colt .38's in the same year.

- **Other Firearms:** These include rifles, submachine guns, and shotguns. The most popular items are the Colt M-16 automatic rifle; the Military Armament Corporation's .380 calibre and 9-mm. submachine guns; and the High Standard Model #10, 12-gauge shotgun. Major sales include 15,000 Colt M-16's to Indonesia in 1979, and another 5,000 M-16's to the Nicaraguan National Guard in 1976. U.S. firms have also sold large quantities of ammunition for these and other firearms.

- **Riot Agents:** These are usually identified as "tear gas," although they are not gases but powdery substances, and one of them, CS, produces much more devastating effects than tearing.* U.S. firms produce CN (chloroaceto-phenone), the original "tear gas" developed by the Army during World War I; and CS (orthochlorobenzalmalono-nitrile), or "pepper gas," which produces coughing, chok-ing, and a burning sensation on the skin. The principal producers are Smith & Wesson and Federal Laboratories, Inc.; both firms package the agents in grenades, shells (for use with shotguns and special riot guns), and in liquid solutions for use with aerosol spray systems. Major buyers include Egypt, which obtained 154,000 tear-gas projectiles of various kinds over the past three years, and Malaysia, which bought 102,000.

- **MACE:** This is a special type of chemical weapon used to incapacitate individuals for periods of up to thirty minutes at a time. MACE consists of an aerosol mixture of CN, kerosene, and solvents which produce tearing, burning

---

*These substances are also described in government documents as "non-lethal munitions" since they do not—in normal concentrations—result in the death of persons exposed to them. However, "tear gas" was known to produce death in Vietnam, where enemy soldiers were sometimes exposed to very high concentrations in their underground shelters. Furthermore, smoke and gas grenades are often discharged at fairly high velocities and thus can kill or maim when fired at demonstrators from close range. In Spain, for instance, a young woman died on January 23, 1977 after being hit on the head by a police smoke-bomb cannister during a student protest in Madrid.[6]

sensations, and dizziness when sprayed on human skin. These weapons were first produced by the General Ordnance Equipment Corp. (a subsidiary of Smith & Wesson) under the trademark "MACE", and this name has become the generic term for all products of this sort.[7] A similar product, the Federal Streamer, is produced by Federal Laboratories.

• **Armored Cars:** The only armored police vehicle currently produced for export is the V-150 "Commando," manufactured by the Cadillac Gage Corp. of Warren, Michigan (a subsidiary of the Ex-Cell-O Corporation). These vehicles normally come equipped with radios, loudspeakers, and gun turrets, and can carry up to twelve policemen. Over 4,000 V-150's have been sold over the past ten years, at an average cost of $100,000.[8] The Detroit police used some during the 1967 riots, but they are not normally employed by U.S. law enforcement agencies; in many Third World countries, however, they are used to crush demonstrations and strikes. Major V-150 customers in recent years have included the police forces of Turkey, Indonesia, Thailand, Malaysia, Panama, Saudi Arabia and the Philippines.

• **Surveillance Devices:** The Vietnam War spurred the development of a great variety of night-vision devices and other surveillance systems for use in jungle operations; now such equipment is beginning to find its way into the arsenals of domestic and foreign forces. The OMC documents list sales of two families of night-vision devices: Smith & Wesson's "Star-tron" system and Javelin Electronic's models #221, #222, and #223. Both systems can be mounted on still or movie cameras (to collect evidence) or on rifles for night combat operations.

Other police products which are in demand abroad but which do not show up on the OMC documents are handcuffs, helmets and shields, riot clubs, electronic surveillance systems, patrol vehicles, and computers. These items are not entered on the Munitions List and thus are not processed through CS channels; instead, they are sold under Commerce Department auspices (see discussion in Chapter 5).

Besides selling arms and equipment, U.S. firms are

increasingly providing training, management support,

and technical assistance to police and intelligence agencies abroad. Smith & Wesson acknowledges that police officials from Finland, the Netherlands, Venezuela, Saudi Arabia and other foreign countries have attended its "Smith & Wesson Academy" in Springfield, Massachusetts during the past few years. According to a company brochure, the academy provides training in such subjects as Firearms and Non-Lethal Weapons, Chemical Munitions Administration, Firearms Instructor, Automatic Weapons Seminar, Police Baton, and Night Surveillance Techniques.[9] Federal Laboratories also admits foreign trainees to its annual "chemical weapons school" in Saltsburg, Pennsylvania, and runs riot-control seminars for law enforcement personnel at selected sites around the world. And, in one of the most outrageous instances of U.S. support for dictators abroad, the Bell Helicopter Company of Ft. Worth, Texas (a division of Textron, Inc.) provided training to several dozen helicopter pilots from Idi Amin's Police Air Wing in 1977 (a program that was discontinued after its exposure in Jack Anderson's newspaper column).[10]

SUPPLIERS

The suppliers of police weaponry tend to be relatively small firms (i.e., when compared to the giant aerospace and shipbuilding companies) which produce specialized gear for the U.S. and foreign police market. Some of these companies—Colt, Remington, and Winchester—can trace their history back to the earliest days of the arms industry in the United States (although in many cases they have since become subsidiaries of large, diversified conglomerates). Because they deal in small arms and other light weapons, these firms rarely participate in the Foreign Military Sales program, but prefer to work through the more permissive CS program. Because so much of their business involves sales to foreign police and security agencies, these firms can truly be called the *merchants of repression.*

By all accounts the giant in this field is the Smith & Wesson Company of Springfield, Mass., a longtime producer of pistols and revolvers. S&W is believed to control 75   **67** percent of the domestic market for standard police hardware, and a substantial share of the international market for such products. The firm was acquired by the Bangor Punta Corp. in 1965, and since then S&W has embarked on an aggressive campaign to buy up small producers of specialized police gear. In 1966, for instance, it acquired the Lake Erie Chemical Co., producers of riot gases, and the General Ordnance Equipment Corp., suppliers of Chemical MACE. As a result of these acquisitions, S&W now provides "the world's longest line of law enforcement products," including handguns, shotguns, chemical agents, MACE, clubs, helmets, handcuffs, and night-vision devices. In addition to its manufacturing activities, S&W also provides training to U.S. and foreign police officers at its Smith & Wesson Academy in Springfield, and at its Armorers School, which provides training in firearms repair and maintenance. Together, the two S&W schools have an annual enrollment of about 1,000 trainees.[11]

After Smith & Wesson, the major U.S. firm in this field is Federal Laboratories, Inc., of Saltsburg, Pa., a subsidiary of the Breeze Corporation. Federal Labs pioneered the development of chemical agents for crowd-control use, and today it is the world's leading producer of these weapons. Federal gained notoriety in the 1930's for its practice of supplying corporations with tear gas for use against striking workers ("it's better to gas a worker than to kill him," Federal's President John W. Young once told a Senate committee[12]), and today the firm still adopts a crusading tone when promoting the use of chemical agents in Third World countries. Spreading tear gas to disperse rioters, one Federal executive told us, "is like using a fumigant to clear the streets."[13] In order to encourage the use of such weapons, Federal Labs runs training seminars for law enforcement personnel in many foreign countries, and convenes an annual chemical weapons school for U.S. and foreign police officers at its headquarters in Pennsylvania.

Other leading producers in the law enforcement field are: Colt Firearms (a subsidiary of Colt Industries, Inc.), manufacturers of handguns and the M-16 rifle; Remington Arms (a subsidiary of DuPont), producers of rifles and ammunition; and Winchester International (a subsidiary of the Olin Corp.), another producer of firearms and ammunition. (See Table XI.) Aside from these manufacturers, the most active firms in the overseas police trade are export firms like Polak, Winters and Company of San Francisco; Jonas Aircraft & Arms Company of New York City; Fargo International of Kensington, Md.; and Technipol International of Foster City, Calif. These firms do not manufacture any products on their own, but serve as trade representatives and export handlers for the smaller producers which lack their own marketing divisions.

More than any other U.S. companies, these arms firms resemble the free-wheeling "merchants of death" of older days in the sense that they aim to sell their products to any government willing and able to produce the necessary cash. Indeed, so eager are they for foreign business that some—like Federal Laboratories—will fly salesmen to foreign capitals in the immediate aftermath of strikes and riots in order to drum up new orders. ("At a glance, I can smell where trouble's brewing in the world," Harry Wells of Federal Labs told the *Asian Wall Street Journal* in 1978. "In my business, that's important."[14]) And while CS transactions of this sort are theoretically subject to the same human rights constraints as FMS sales, these firms apparently have little compunction about circumventing such restrictions when the opportunity arises.

Perhaps the most blatant example of such duplicity involves illegal arms sales to South Africa. In accordance with the U.N. embargo of 1963, U.S. firms are barred from selling firearms and other Munitions List items to that country. This ban has not, however, prevented some U.S. firms—including Colt and Winchester—from selling arms to "dummy" corporations elsewhere, which then "tranship" the contraband to South African buyers. Such transactions probably could have gone undetected for years, if the firms involved hadn't gotten overly greedy and began pumping huge quantities of arms through improbable transshipment points like the Canary Islands and Botswana. In 1976, an employee of Colt Industries was sentenced to one year in prison for arranging such deliveries, and in 1978 Olin-Winchester was fined $510,000 for similar offenses. In both cases, company officials argued that these practices were widespread in the in-

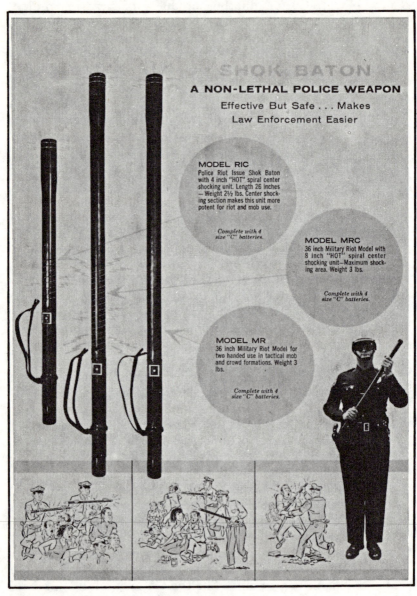

Promotional literature for the "Shok Baton."

201Z Gas Gun

Weighing only 7¼ pounds and only 29" long, this gun fires all 1½" caliber Federal projectiles and cartridges. It is made of high strength alloy which will not rust even with long, hard use. For accurate shooting, the gun has a custom fitted stock and full pistol grip. A flat top front sight and rear peep sight insure accuracy at ranges of 50, 75, and 100 yards. The top opening breech lock and double action trigger make this the fastest firing gun available.
010A005 GAS GUN, 10 LBS. $135.00

Chemical Munitions

MINIMUM ORDER $20

010A032

010A034

010A036

010A084

010C004

203 Federal Short Range Cartridge

This Federal cartridge was developed for use in close up situations where one or two seconds could mean the difference. Unlike other cartridges and projectiles there is no fuze action or delay in the gas release of this cartridge. It blasts right out of the gun barrel in a large cloud that covers a 45 x 25 foot area in 1 second.
010A032 203 SHORT RANGE CART., CN, 1 LB. $8.90
010A033 530 SHORT RANGE CART., CS, 1 LB. $8.90

206 & 219 Federal Spedeheat Projectile

These 1½" caliber projectiles fire from the Federal 201Z Gas Gun. They are best used against crowds in an open area. The projectile is ignited by a delayed fuze 2 seconds after it leaves the barrel of the gun. Gas is released for a period of 25 to 35 seconds. The tumbling, combustion action during flight make pick up and throwback virtually impossible. It is not recommended for use in areas where fire hazard is a threat.
010A034 206 LONG RANGE (150 YDS.) PROJ., CN, 1 LB. $12.80
010A035 560 LONG RANGE (150 YDS.) PROJ., CS, 1 LB. $12.80
010A036 219 SHORT RANGE (70 YDS.) PROJ., CN, 1 LB. $12.80
010A037 570 SHORT RANGE (70 YDS.) PROJ., CS, 1 LB. $12.80

207 Low Recoil Riot Projectile

Designed after Federal's popular 206 Projectile, this economical model has a maximum range of 120 yards. Although it is capable of being fired from all types of 1½" (37-38MM) riot guns, its lightweight, low recoil construction makes it feasible to be fired from 1½" riot pistols as well. Once launched from a riot gun or riot pistol, a delayed fuze of 2 seconds will ignite the charge and the projectile will emit CN or CS smoke for approximately 30 seconds. Due to fire hazards, this projectile is not recommended for use indoors or in confined areas.
010A084 207 LOW RECOIL PROJ., CN, 1 LB. $10.25
010A085 561 LOW RECOIL PROJ., CS, 1 LB. $10.25

37MM Barricade Penetrating Cartridge

This cartridge can be fired from any 37 or 38MM gun instantly releasing a 25 CC non-burning formulation of irritant agent sufficient to incapacitate an individual in a 4500 cubic foot enclosure. The 37MM Cartridge can penetrate a car windshield at 100 ft. and a double panel storm window at 300 ft.
010C004 37MM CARTRIDGE, CN, ¼ LB. $12.00
910C005 37MM CARTRIDGE, CS, ¼ LB. $12.00

FARGO INTERNATIONAL a division of GEOFFREY OBERDICK INC. • PO Box 49, Kensington, Maryland 20795

An ad from the Fargo International Police Equipment Catalog.

TABLE XI:
Arms Sales to Third World Police and Security Forces by Selected U.S. Companies, September 1976 - May 1979[1]

Manufacturer	Gas Grenades & Projectiles	Gas Guns	Cannisters MACE	Rifles & Carbines	Pistols & Revolvers	Ammunition (1000 rds.)
AAI Corp.	5,100					
Browning Arms					15,000	20
Colt Industries				49,469	22,691	52
Federal Cartridge	1,770					1,441
Federal Labs	585,551	3,021				26
Remington Arms				856		8,691
Smith & Wesson[2]	25,316	119	8,695		90,854	3,427
Winchester International		284		284		41,895

1. Source: Licenses issued by the Office of Munitions Control, U.S. Department of State.
2. Includes sales by the General Ordnance Equipment Co., a subsidiary.

dustry and that OMC officials routinely "acquiesced" to such transactions by "looking the other way" when presented with obviously fraudulent applications for export licenses.*[15]

In recent years, U.S. firms have been charged with smuggling arms and related hardware to other countries on the embargo list, including the Libyan Arab Republic. In 1978, for instance, Smith & Wesson was fined $120,000 for selling large quantities of "Star-tron" night-vision scopes to the Libyan military via dealers in France and West Germany.[17] Other U.S. firms have been implicated in similar sales to Socialist-bloc countries of Eastern Europe.

Even in the absence of such illicit operations, it is obvious that these firms are contributing on a regular basis to the repressive capabilities of authoritarian regimes abroad. Because they deal primarily in internal security hardware, and because they sell to the agencies most directly involved in political repression, their activities should be subject to especially careful scrutiny. Yet, as we have seen, such sales are routinely approved by government authorities. Because Commercial Sales transactions are likely to receive even more lenient treatment under the Reagan Administration, it is more than ever essential that such exports be subject to tough and explicit human rights restrictions, and that OMC operations be subject to close public and Congressional scrutiny.

---

*Lawyers for Olin-Winchester, for instance, told a Federal judge in New Haven that "Whatever the actual policy of the U.S. Government was during this period, the Winchester employees principally responsible for dealing with the State Department on export license matters over the years developed the belief that the Department was 'winking' at the representation that arms sent to South Africa were [ostensibly] destined for other countries."[16] Olin ultimately pleaded *nolo contendere* (no contest) to charges that it smuggled 3,200 firearms and 20 million rounds of ammunition to South Africa via dummy firms in Austria, Greece, West Germany, Mozambique and the Canary Islands.

V.

THE 'GRAY AREA' TRADE IN REPRESSION:

POLICE EXPORTS THROUGH COMMERCE DEPARTMENT CHANNELS

Besides the FMS and Commercial Sales programs, there is still *another* channel through which arms and related hardware can be sold to Third World security forces: the conventional trade programs supervised by the Department of Commerce.* Among the items which can be exported this way are transport planes and trainer aircraft, search radars, helicopter engines, computers, and a wide range of "crime control and detection equipment." Although widely used for military purposes, such products are not considered "implements of war" by the Department of State; thus they do not appear on the U.S. Munitions List and do not require processing by the Office of Munitions Control. Because they fall into a murky area between purely military and purely civilian equipment (and can be used for both purposes), these products are known as "dual-use" items or, more descriptively, as "gray-area" hardware. But however ambiguous

---

*Because it is easy to confuse "Commercial Sales" and "Commerce Department channels," let us take a minute to illuminate the differences. "Commercial Sales" refers to exports of military hardware on the U.S. Munitions List through *State Department* channels (specifically, under supervision of the Office of Munitions Control); "Commerce Department channels" refers to exports of standard trade goods under *Commerce Department* auspices. Commercial Sales only involve items on the Munitions List; military-related hardware not on that list fall under Commerce Department jurisdiction.

the designation of such equipment, there is no questioning the fact that it can play a key role in facilitating repression abroad.

The Commerce Department oversees a very wide variety of exported products, most of which have no direct application to military activities. Among the many classifications of U.S. trade goods, however, are a number of categories which are revelant to our discussion. These include: "crime control and detection equipment"; "non-military arms"; "non-military" aircraft, aircraft engines, and radars; and electronic computers. In this chapter, we will examine these categories and the role they play in overseas police activities.

CRIME CONTROL AND DETECTION EQUIPMENT

Among the many categories of manufactured goods listed in the Commerce Department's directory of trade classifications is "Crime Control and Detection Equipment." This category encompasses such items as: "non-military arms such as shotguns, stun guns, dart guns, riot guns, and shock batons." Also, "straight-jackets, non-military gas masks, bullet-proof vests and shields," and "non-military protective vests, leg irons, shackles, handcuffs, thumbscrews, and other manufactures of metal."[1]

Just how much of any particular item is sold to any particular government is difficult to determine, both because of the reporting procedures involved and because of the pervasive secrecy which enshrouds most Commerce Department operations. Prior to 1978, U.S. firms could export items in the "crime control" category to almost all non-communist countries without first obtaining a "validated license" from the Commerce Department; instead, exporters operated under a so-called "general license," a sort of blanket authority for unsupervised exports to Western nations and Third World allies. Compounding the lack of formal documentation (such as the export licenses issued by the Office of Munitions Control which were used to prepare the tables in Chapter 4), the Census Bureau—which compiles trade statistics for the Department of Commerce—

lumps police hardware together with meat hooks and other miscellaneous items under the heading, "Articles, not elsewhere classified, of iron and steel." Accordingly, one can only speculate as to how many thumbscrews were included in the $1.7 million worth of hardware Chile purchased in this category between 1974 and 1976. Or how many leg irons and shackles South Africa acquired among its purchases of $2.4 million.[2]

Sales of "non-military arms" and ammunition are somewhat easier to track, since the Census Bureau maintains a separate category for such equipment in its monthly statistical reports on U.S. trade. According to these reports, U.S. firms sold 69,776 "non-military shotguns" to customers in Thailand during the year preceding the bloody coup of October 1976, and another 2,435 firearms to Nicaragua during the last two years of Somoza's dictatorship. Other customers for such weapons include Uruguay, which bought 400 shotguns in the first few months of 1977 alone (despite a total Congressional ban on military aid and FMS sales), and South Africa, which bought more than 1,000 shotguns over the 18-month period ending in September, 1977.[3]

Another troubling category of hardware listed by the Census Bureau is "non-military arms, not elsewhere specified." This category includes such items as blackjacks, truncheons, billy clubs and similar items of this character. Recipients of such equipment, according to Census Bureau trade reports, include Iran (under the Shah), Indonesia, Saudi Arabia, Brazil and the Dominican Republic. And despite the arms embargo on South Africa, U.S. firms sold $300,000 worth of such weapons to that country between January 1976 and September 1977.[4]

When these statistics were first revealed by one of the authors in the *Los Angeles Times* in April, 1978,[5] many readers were understandably skeptical that any U.S. companies produced—let alone exported—items like thumbscrews, leg irons, truncheons, and shock-batons which could so easily be used for torture. Yet, in examining the catalogs issued by U.S. security firms, we found examples of virtually all of these goods. The Technipol International Corp. of Foster City, California, for instance, freely advertises a wide selection of "restraint equipment" including leg-irons, shackles, and "thumbcuffs." Several major suppliers, including Smith & Wesson, produce a variety of clubs, billies and truncheons for export. Finally, the Shok Baton Company of Savage, Minnesota—also home of the Hot-Shot Company, producers of cattle prods—manufactures the Electric "Shok-Baton," a billy-club fitted with an electric shock device which can deliver up to 600 volts on contact.[6] All of these items can, and no doubt have, been used to violate human rights. Thus the Danish Medical Group of Amnesty International, which found the Shok-Baton in use in Cyprus and elsewhere, tested the device on volunteers and reported: "the instrument studied . . . can, under the given experimental conditions, cause pain described by five out of six volunteers as severe, [and by two] as intolerable."*[7]

Following the publication of the 1978 article in the *Los Angeles Times,* Congress adopted an amendment to the Foreign Assistance Act tightening the regulations governing the export of non-military weapons and equipment to the Third World. Known as the "thumbscrew amendment," the measure required that all crime control and detection equipment exports to Third World countries be fully licensed, and reviewed in advance by the State Department's Office of Human Rights and Humanitarian Affairs. Shortly after its passage, however, the measure was undermined by an amendment to the Export Administration Act of 1979, which gave the Executive Branch broad authority to exempt friendly countries from the special licensing procedures, and assured that license applications, where required, would be concealed from public scrutiny on the grounds that they contain "proprietary business information."

*"Colonel" Rex Applegate, a consultant on riot-control techniques, once wrote that "the shock-baton has been one of the least understood and most maligned weapons available to law enforcement...It is being used in quantity by paramilitary police abroad . . . The harmless shock delivered has a great psychological as well as practical deterrent effect. . . Its usefulness in sit-down, passive-resistance, and campus riot situations is obvious but has yet to be fully explored."[8]

COMPUTERS

If the Commerce Department is determined to hide security exports from public scrutiny, it is even more secretive in the case of computer exports. Asked, under the Freedom of Information Act, to supply information on the sale of U.S. computers to foreign police forces in 1977, then Secretary of Commerce Juanita Kreps refused on the grounds that such disclosure could "expose many of these firms to pressure by various individuals and groups that disagree with the government's decision to authorize exports" to certain foreign governments (i.e., dictatorships), and thus disrupt "normal export trade patterns" at a time when exports should be increased.[9] Despite such concealment, however, it is possible to show that U.S. computers have been sold to foreign police and security agencies, including those in countries ruled by authoritarian regimes.

According to a reputable trade journal, *Computer Decisions,* U.S. computers are used by intelligence agencies in several Latin American countries to keep track of dissidents and to pinpoint individuals for arrest, interrogation, and, on occasion, for assassination. In May 1975, for instance, General Pinochet of Chile dedicated an IBM 370/145 computer at the Technical University in Santiago; although industry officials insisted that the computer would be used for payroll and other routine purposes, *Computer Decisions* reported that the IBM 370/145 at the Technical University was linked to a computer network serving Chile's secret police and other government agencies.[10] Similar networks, in turn, are reportedly linked to systems in other "Southern Cone" countries, including Argentina, Brazil and Uruguay.*

---

*One such operation, code-named CONDOR and centered in Chile, linked intelligence agencies in the Southern Cone of Latin America. According to a U.S. official, " . . . CONDOR is the code name for the collection, exchange, and storage of intelligence data concerning leftists, communists, and Marxists . . . in order to eliminate Marxist terrorists and their activities in the area." A secret phase of CONDOR involved the "formation of special teams . . . to carry out sanctions [including] assassinations." The murder of Chilean exile leader Orlando Letelier was a CONDOR operation.[11]

Other U.S. computers have been sold to security forces throughout Latin America, where there appears to be a growing market for such wares.* Thus E-Systems of Dallas, Texas—a major provider of secret electronic and radio equipment to the CIA and Pentagon (and developer of the "electronic warfare" equipment used in Vietnam)—boasted of the "delivery and installation of the largest, most complex [police computer] system to date" in Argentina. Inaugurated in 1977, the E-Systems' "Digicom" complex in Buenos Aires provides, according to the company's promotional brochures, "officers in the field with immediate, intelligible data on critical situations and [gives] them a direct communications link from vehicles to local, regional, and national data files." The Digicom System features Mobile Digital Terminals installed in individual police cars, which are connected to central police dispatchers and the government's central data base and intelligence files.[12]

E-Systems claims that the Digicom complex allows police to "get through instantly and get quick replies in checking license numbers, driver's licenses, and other needed information."[13] In a country like Argentina, where thousands of dissidents have disappeared, or been kidnapped and tortured by security forces, the E-Systems facility helps, as *Computer Decisions* put it, to "automate the 'final solution.'"[14]

Sensitive to the human rights implications of the Digicom system, in 1978 the State Department denied E-Systems a license to furnish Argentina with $7 million worth of equipment to link the network in Buenos Aires with similar systems in nineteen other cities. In a letter to E-Systems in March, Deputy Secretary of State Warren Christopher stated that "our continuing deep concern over the serious human rights situation precludes our approval of the export of this equipment."[15] However, the Carter

---

*To a large extent, this demand has been stimulated by earlier U.S. grants of such hardware under the Public Safety program. OPS deliveries to Brazil, for instance, included a $137,000 IBM information-processing system, while Venezuela was given an electronic "war room" for its central police headquarters in Caracas. Computerized intelligence systems have also been supplied to Latin American countries under the International Narcotics Control program (see Chapter 2).

Administration's record on other computer sales shows, at best, an ambivalence toward the human rights impact of such advanced technology.

In 1978, for example, the U.S. government granted a license to Rockwell International for the sale of a computerized fingerprint identification system to Brazil's military regime. The Rockwell "Printrak 250," delivered to the Brazilian states of Sao Paulo, Brasilia, and Bahia, formed the nucleus of a national identification system designed to extend eventually to the entire country. By storing fingerprint data in a disc-type memory bank, the Printrak computer can process new fingerprints fed into the system, producing the name, address, and background information on a given individual. Other electronic gear allows the system to "call up" other computers for additional information.[16]

EVADING THE EMBARGOES: 'GRAY AREA' SALES TO SOUTH AFRICA AND CHILE

In addition to serving as a conduit for exports of security gear and computers to Third World police forces, Commerce Department channels are also used by U.S. corporations (usually with U.S. Government acquiescence) to circumvent embargoes on sales to particular regimes, including such major violators of human rights as South Africa and Chile. While U.S. laws and regulations ban the sale of standard combat gear—tanks, missiles, fighter planes, etc.—to these countries, they do not explicitly prohibit sales of "dual-use" combat-support equipment—trainer aircraft and transport planes, search radars, communications gear, etc.—and thus U.S. officials have often interpreted the embargo to permit transfers of such hardware through the Department of Commerce. Such exports are often considerable—U.S. aircraft firms, for instance, sold hundreds of millions of dollars worth of aviation equipment to South Africa in the 1960s and 1970s—are are likely to increase under the Reagan Administration.

The ban on arms exports to South Africa has been in
effect since August 1963, when the United States agreed to a

United Nations Security Council Resolution (No. 181) calling for such actions. Although all U.S. presidents since John F. Kennedy have upheld the ban, and while it has been largely effective in blocking sales of standard combat gear (i.e., items on the U.S. Munitions List), there has always been considerable vacillation in the extent to which it was applied to support-type equipment. During the Johnson Administration, the measure was interpreted as covering any item with a potential military use, but President Nixon—under prodding from then Secretary of State Kissinger—adopted a far more permissive stance on this question.[17] As specified in National Security Decision Memorandum 38 (NSDM-38), Nixon determined that the United States would "enforce the arms embargo against South Africa, but with liberal treatment of equipment which could serve either military or civilian purposes."[18] On the basis of this principle, Washington authorized the sale of six Lockheed L-100 cargo planes (the "civilian" equivalent of the C-130 "Hercules" military transport) and seven Swearingen "Merlin-IV" medium transports to the South African Air Force (SAAF); together with other aircraft sales, these transactions pushed total U.S. aviation exports to South Africa from a rate of $30 million per year in the late 1960s to $170 million annually between 1974 and 1976.[19]

Soon after President Carter took office, the uprising in Soweto—and resulting government crackdown—focused new attention on South Africa, and prompted the United Nations to adopt a new, tougher arms embargo (Security Council Resolution 418). In line with the U.N. action, Carter banned the sale of *any* item, whatever its purpose, to South African military and police forces. But while this measure has largely stopped the export of gray-area equipment to the military, it has not prevented the sale of dual-use equipment to *non-military* groups and agencies in South Africa— including many organizations which work closely with the military or are in fact "dummy" institutions set up specifically to circumvent the embargo. Thus many of the light planes sold to individuals and corporations in South Africa are reportedly used by the "Air Commandos," an all-white, voluntary militia of businessmen who fly their own aircraft on support missions for the SAAF.[20] Despite widespread evidence of such subterfuge, the Carter Administration approved the sale of some 70 to 80 Cessna and Piper light planes to South Africa in March 1978, a month after the new ban came into effect.[21] Subsequent disclosures, involving the sale of Control Data Corporation computers and Sanders Associates surveillance gear to quasi-military agencies in South Africa, indicate that significant quantities of combat-support gear are continuing to reach that country through Commerce Department channels.[22]

Turning to Chile, we find a similar pattern of collusion. Shortly after Congress voted in 1976 to ban all FMS and Commercial Sales exports to the Pinochet regime, the Carter Administration approved the sale of four Swearingen "Metro-II" transport planes to the Carabineros (Chile's military police force) through Commerce Department channels. The Chilean military has also been able to purchase several Beech "King Air" turboprop transports and eighteen Cessna light planes through Commerce.[23] Moreover, U.S. powerplants and surveillance systems have also been incorporated into military aircraft sold to Chile by firms in Brazil.* In 1976, for instance, Brazil's EMBRAER (Empresa Brasileira de Aeronautica) factory delivered to the Chilean Navy six EMB-111M "Bandeirante" naval patrol planes equipped with a U.S. AN/APS-128 search radar manufactured by the Cutler-Hammer Co. of Deer Park, New York. The AN/APS-128 military radars were initially embargoed by U.S. officials, but subsequently delivered when Cutler-Hammer agreed to "civilianize" the system with government assistance, thereby permitting export through Commerce Department channels.[24] Another Brazilian firm, Neiva, has sold the Chilean Air Force eighteen T-12 "Universal" trainer planes powered by Avco-Lycoming IO-540 piston engines (aircraft engines of this type are not on

---

*Such "third-country transfers," involving sales of U.S. components and/or technology to foreign arms producers which then sell a completed weapon to yet another country, are becoming increasingly frequent. Theoretically, such sales are subject to the same regulations and restrictions that govern direct U.S. sales to the ultimate recipient, but such transactions are inherently difficult to monitor and are generally handled with greater leniency by U.S. officials, with the result that they have become a favored ploy for U.S. firms seeking to sell their products to countries on the embargo list.

the Munitions List and thus can be exported under Commerce Department aegis).[25]

Already a major conduit for the export of arms and related hardware to Third World police and security forces, the Commerce Department is likely to move even more such goods in the 1980s.* Under new guidelines adopted toward the end of Carter's term, the State Department lost its authority to review Commerce-supervised sales of security gear to police and military agencies abroad. (Under the new procedures, the President can designate certain specialized *items* for State Department review—but not, as in the past, particular countries or *end-users*—and until now security equipment and light aircraft have not been so designated.) And given Ronald Reagan's desire to boost U.S. trade—and his critical attitude towards Carter's human rights policy— it is likely that Washington will further dilute all remaining constraints on the export of security-type hardware to authoritarian regimes abroad. If the Nixon experience is any indication, moreover, Reagan will again relax the interpretation of the 1963 U.N. embargo in order to permit increased sales of gray-area equipment to South Africa. It is obvious, therefore, that any new effort to curb U.S. support for repression abroad will have to encompass these Commerce Department channels as well as the more familiar arms programs administered by the Departments of State and Defense.

---

*Indeed, the Commerce Department has been actively promoting U.S. exports of repression hardware. In May 1980, the Department sponsored a "Security 80" exposition at the U.S. International Marketing Center in Paris. Many leading U.S. suppliers displayed their wares at the show, including Technipol International, Federal Laboratories, and Fargo International.[26]

VI.

CONCLUSION:

THE REPRESSION TRADE AFTER CARTER

After examining all the evidence presented in the previous chapters, there is no escaping the conclusion that the United States, its government, and its arms industry have been deeply involved in the supply of repressive technology to authoritarian regimes abroad. In many documented cases, moreover, this hardware has been supplied directly to the state security agencies most directly involved in political terrorism. President Carter did not invent this "repression pipeline," nor the policies that justify it; however, by failing to re-evaluate the "national security" ideology that has governed U.S. foreign policy since World War II, Mr. Carter insured that the pipeline remained intact, while U.S. efforts on behalf of human rights remained at a relatively modest level.

The publicity given to human rights by the Carter Administration did, on occasion, make a real difference. U.S. pressure on some regimes led to the release of some political prisoners, and a reduction (usually temporary) in the level of violence against dissidents. In 1977, moreover, U.S. criticism prompted several Latin American governments—including Argentina, Brazil, El Salvador, and Guatemala—to reject further U.S. military assistance. Washington also refrained from sending military aid to Nicaraguan dictator Anastasio Somoza during his final struggle against the Sandinistas. These moves were greeted with much enthusiasm by human rights activists abroad, and helped remove some of the stigma Washington bore at home because of Vietnam. More often than not, however, Carter spoke out more vigorously against human rights abuses in the Soviet Union and Eastern Europe than against those in Third World dictatorships where the United States had historically contributed to repression, thus using human rights to promote a new Cold War.

In looking back, moreover, it should be noted that a human rights policy did not originate in the White House, but was rather a product of Congressional action and public pressure which pre-dated the Carter Administration. And while Carter readily appropriated this policy when it proved convenient, his enthusiasm often evaporated when it conflicted with other policy goals. Indeed, the Administration viewed legislation that linked foreign assistance to human rights practices as unwarranted interference in foreign policy decision-making, and so Carter consistently opposed Congressional efforts to tighten existing laws which prohibit military and economic aid to governments cited for "gross and consistent" violations of human rights.

Furthermore, in the final years of his Administration, Carter abandoned much of his earlier commitment to human rights and began stepping up arms deliveries to many repressive governments, including those in Indonesia, Thailand, the Philippines, South Korea, El Salvador and Morocco. And when favored Third World regimes were threatened by internal upheaval—Iran and Guatemala in 1978, Tunisia and El Salvador in 1980—Carter did not hesitate to send emergency shipments of anit-riot equipment and other weapons used by government forces to suppress dissent.[1] On balance, therefore, it appears that while Carter did reduce weapons sales to a few small countries—Nicaragua being a prominent example—for the most part human rights considerations played only a minor role in governing U.S. arms exports to repressive Third World regimes.

Indeed, by the end of Carter's term, it could well be asked if the Administration had a human rights policy at all. On the eve of Reagan's inauguration, the Pentagon rushed shipments of helicopters and other lethal combat equipment to El Salvador, where government forces had killed thousands of unarmed Salvadoreans—as well as several U.S. citizens—in a bloody effort to contain popular rebellion. Carter also dispatched counter-insurgency advisers and other U.S. military personnel to El Salvador, thus paving the way for escalating U.S. military involvement in Central America.[2]

Admittedly, the web of laws and regulations governing military exports is exceedingly complex, and Carter did make an effort to rationalize some aspects of the arms transfer process (an effort that is now being reversed by the Reagan Administration). But so long as Washington remains committed to the existing alliance system, and continues to view all Third World turmoil through the distorted prism of superpower conflict, there can be little easing of the momentum behind arms sales and repressive exports. Indeed, given Reagan's commitment to restore U.S. "superiority," and to rebuild U.S. ties with "moderately repressive"[3] allies in the Third World, we can expect a substantial increase in such exports. Indeed, in receiving President Chun of South Korea as one of the first foreign heads-of-state to visit the White House under the new Administration, President Reagan indicated that Washington would no longer pressure Seoul on human rights issues ("What happens internally is an internal affair of the Republic of Korea," a State Department official told reporters at a White House briefing on the Chun visit), but would rather concentrate on building up South Korea's military capabilities.[4]

While we cannot predict every step the new Administration is likely to take, several observations can be made regarding the probable direction of Reagan's foreign and military policies. Mentioned here are the Reagan initiatives which will have the greatest bearing on human rights behavior abroad; as can be readily seen, many of these will also have a profound impact on the political environment in the United States, as well.

• *Increased military spending,* coupled with a growing propensity to intervene in Third World conflicts which appear to bear on U.S. economic and security interests. Reagan is expected to add $30-35 billion to the $190 billion defense budget proposed by Mr. Carter for Fiscal Year 1982, and to add another $40 billion in each of the succeeding four years. This increment will be used to enhance the combat "readiness" of U.S. armed forces, and to expand the newly-formed Rapid Deployment Force (RDF)—a sort of global "S.W.A.T. team" for suppressing Third World disorders.

• *Increased arms sales,* involving a substantial expansion of the Foreign Military Sales program along with the abrogation of all the restraints imposed by Mr. Carter in 1977. Total FMS sales, which reached a near-record $15.3 billion in Fiscal 1980 while the Carter restraints were still in force, will undoubtedly reach new heights in the years ahead.

• *Increased support for pro-U.S. regimes abroad,* including many Third World governments which have been subjected to military aid cuts because of their atrocious record on human rights. Such support is likely to include arms credits, grants of training and equipment, and the deployment of U.S. advisers and counter-insurgency specialists. Administration officials have repeatedly mentioned South Korea, Guatemala and El Salvador as countries meriting strong U.S. support, and increased aid can also be expected for such countries as Thailand, Indonesia, the Philippines, Taiwan, Morocco, and Oman. And, in one of his first official acts, Secretary of State Haig asked Congress to lift its embargo on U.S. military sales to Argentina—despite reports of continuing mistreatment of political prisoners in that country.[5]

• *Increased employment of covert operations* against foreign governments, organizations, and individuals abroad. This is likely to include stepped-up U.S. cooperation with foreign police and intelligence services, including many which have been implicated in the systematic violation of individual human rights, as well as direct destabilization efforts against "hostile" regimes. The Reagan Administration has also asked Congress to lift restrictions on U.S. covert military operations in Angola.

• *The relaxation of controls on non-governmental arms export channels,* including the Commercial Sales program administered by the Department of State, and "gray area" sales administered by the Department of Commerce. This will also involve relaxed oversight of "third-country transfers" (involving the sale of U.S. components and/or technology to foreign arms

87

producers which then sell complete weapons systems to still other countries), and arms "co-production" projects (involving the joint manufacture of weapons by U.S. and foreign firms). These moves are likely to facilitate arms shipments to countries now on the embargoed list, including Chile and South Africa.

• *The increased "privatization" of the repression trade,* involving official encouragement for stepped-up corporate sales of security systems and services. This will probably result in the expansion of private police schools like the Smith & Wesson Academy, as well as increased sales of security services by private guard companies. Among the latter are Pinkerton's, the Wackenhut Corporation, and William J. Burns International Security Services—all of which have expanded their foreign operations in the past few years."*

In addition to these initiatives, there is the danger that Reagan will seek to roll back existing legislation governing human rights and arms exports. Indeed, Reagan's first choice for Assistant Secretary of State for Human Rights and Humanitarian Affairs, Ernest W. Lefever, testified in 1979 that "the United States should remove from the statute books all clauses that establish a human rights standard or condition that must be met by another sovereign government before our government transacts normal business with it."[7] Especially vulnerable are those measures prohibiting U.S. aid and training for Third World police forces, and restrictions on military exports to particular countries such as Chile and Argentina. It is also possible that Secretary of State Haig will attempt to revise elements of the defunct Public Safety program in the guise of assisting Third World govern-

---

*These firms typically sell their services to U.S.-based multinational corporations with extensive holdings in the Third World. Wackenhut, for instance, employs over 1,200 security guards in Brazil, and comparable numbers in Colombia, Ecuador, Venezuela, and the Dominican Republic. Some U.S. firms, such as Intertel (International Intelligence, Inc.), also run private intelligence organizations staffed by former operatives of the CIA, FBI, and military intelligence. Major consumers of such services include the large oil, mining, and agribusiness companies, as well as banks and communications firms.[6]

ments to combat "international terrorism." Finally, in the name of "national security," there is every likelihood that the Reagan Administration will turn back the clock to pre-Vietnam days, when American commitments to unpopular rulers led to deepening involvement in the internal affairs of foreign nations.

In recognition of this danger, 72 prominent religious leaders from all over the country told Reagan in December 1980 that "there is increasing and alarming evidence that military governments in many countries are viewing your election as a green light for suppression of legitimate dissent, and for widespread arrest and imprisonment, torture, and murder." In their letter to the president-elect, these leaders, including twelve bishops, asserted that " . . . from your record and stands we judge that you would not condone such erosion of democratic rights, nor would the great majority of those Americans who elected you, for it is only on the foundation of such rights and not on violent repression, that a just and lasting peace can be built."[8]

Despite such appeals, Reagan is certain to downplay human rights in favor of the timeworn prerogatives of "national security" and U.S.-Soviet competition. And if recent history is any indication, the Administration is likely to find many opportunities to assist foreign dictators against their domestic opponents. The repression pipeline, already jammed with new equipment for favored Third World regimes, will soon be enlarged to accommodate all the additional hardware promised by the Reagan Administration.

But despite this effort to resuscitate the discredited policies of the Cold War era, U.S. aid will not produce the stability and security sought by Washington. U.S. assistance may prolong the tenure of selected dictatorships, but it cannot address the political, social and economic inequities which produce dissent in the first place. More often than not, the only lasting result of political repression is the abandonment of public protest by dissidents in favor of more militant, underground activities. Indeed, history shows that it is the *denial* of fundamental human rights that ultimately ensures that opposition forces will turn to armed rebellion in their efforts to promote meaningful change—and it is only through the satisfaction of basic human rights that we can be assured of lasting world stability. As former Secretary of State Cyrus Vance noted in his 1980 commencement address at Harvard University, "we must ultimately recognize that the demand for individual freedom and economic progress cannot be long repressed without sowing the seeds of violent convulsion. Thus ... we have a stake in the stability that comes when people can express their hopes and build their futures freely."[9]

Clearly, the supply of repressive technology and the promotion of human rights are wholly incompatible. If we are genuinely committed to the advancement of fundamental human rights abroad, we must dismantle the repression pipeline that provides so much aid and comfort to foreign dictatorships. Specifically, we must:

- Ban the export of *any* item which can be used for the torture, assassination, mistreatment, or injury of political dissidents;
- Restrict the delivery of military hardware and services to any government cited for consistent violations of internationally-recognized human rights;
- Discontinue the training of foreign police, paramilitary, and internal security forces in the United States or at U.S. facilities abroad;
- Require that all police and military exports through State Department and Commerce Department channels be examined for their impact on the human rights situation in recipient countries, with automatic rejection of any sales to countries with a consistent pattern of abuse;
- And, finally, resist any effort to relax or eliminate existing restraints on the export of military technology to foreign dictatorships.

These steps will not halt the abuse of human rights abroad. But they will weaken the capacity of foreign security forces to suppress dissent, and serve notice that the United States will no longer come to the rescue of authoritarian regimes threatened by popular revolt. More importantly, they will reinvigorate our own democratic rights by ending U.S. involvement in the denial of such rights abroad.

Alongside the moral and policy imperatives for such

action, there is also a grave penalty for *in*action: the certainty that the pipeline of repression will increasingly carry a *reverse flow* of political violence. For, by becoming involved in the creation and nourishment of authoritarian systems abroad, we cannot hope to escape their ravages at home. Already, the governments of South Korea, Iran, and Chile have sent their minions to the United States to pervert our institutions (including even Congress itself) or to murder our citizens and guests (as in the case of the assassination of Orlando Letelier and Ronni Moffitt in Washington on September 21, 1976).[10] And the U.S.-supported security forces of El Salvador have been implicated in the murder of Maura Clarke, Ita Ford, Jean Donovan, and Dorothy Kazel, American churchwomen working in that country. If we are to protect our own citizens, freedoms and liberties from the *reverse flow* of barbarism, we must halt the *export* of repression to foreign governments.

The world is becoming too complex, the actors too numerous and their goals too diverse, for the United States to continue to impose its political will on foreign societies. A policy of non-involvement in the internal affairs of other countries has been a consistent, if oft-neglected feature of American policy since Washington's inauguration; it is a principle that we more than ever need to follow today. At a minimum, this policy should preclude any form of support for the police or internal security forces of another government. Even more important, the principle of non-intervention must be rigidly enforced if we are to avoid entanglement in another Vietnam—or worse, a series of "police actions" that would bankrupt our country morally as well as economically.

FOOTNOTES

Chapter 1

1. Quoted in *The New York Times,* March 18 and May 23, 1977.

2. Quoted in *The New York Times,* April 15, 1977.

3. Quoted in *The Washington Post,* January 29, 1981.

4. Quoted in "Reagan and Human Rights," *Newsweek* (December 15, 1979), p. 53.

5. Quoted in *The New York Times,* February 24, 1977.

6. For background on the human rights performance of individual countries, see: the *Amnesty International Report,* published annually by Amnesty International in London; the Amnesty International *Report on Torture* (New York: Farrar, Straus, Giroux, 1975); individual Amnesty International country reports; U.S. Department of State, *Country Reports on Human Rights Practices,* published annually in compliance with Section 502(b) of the Foreign Assistance Act; hearings on human rights conditions in specific countries held by the Subcommittee on International Organizations of the House Committee on International Relations; and individual country reports issued by the International Commission of Jurists in Geneva and the Inter-American Human Rights Commission of the Organization of American States in Washington, D.C.

7. Fiscal Years 1976-80 data: U.S. Defense Security Assistance Agency, *Foreign Military Sales and Military Assistance Facts* (Washington, D.C., 1979), pp. 1-37 (hereinafter cited as: DSAA, *FMS/MAP Facts 1979*). Fiscal 1981 data: U.S. Department of Defense, *Congressional Presentation Document, Security Assistance Program,* Fiscal Year 1981 (Washington, D.C., 1980), pp. 1-35 (hereinafter cited as: DoD, *Security Assistance Program FY81*).

8. For a full-scale discussion of the underlying motives which govern U.S. military aid policy, see: Noam Chomsky and Edward S. Herman, *The Political Economy of Human Rights,* Vol. I (Boston: South End Press, 1979).

9. U.S. Agency for International Development, *U.S. Overseas Loans and Grants, July 1, 1945-September 30, 1979* (Washington, D.C., 1980), p. 6 (hereinafter cited as: USAID, *U.S. Loans and Grants, 1945-79*).

10. Edwin Lieuwen, "The Latin American Military," in U.S. Congress, Senate, Committee on Foreign Relations, Subcommittee on American Republics Affairs, *Survey of the Alliance for Progress,* Compilation of Studies and Hearings (Washington, D.C.: Government Printing Office, 1969), p. 115.

11. U.S. Congress, House, Committee on Foreign Affairs, *Foreign Assistance Act of 1967,* Hearings, 90th Cong., 1st Sess., 1967, p. 117. For further discussion of Kennedy's counterinsurgency priorities, see: Douglas S. Blaufarb, *The Counterinsurgency Era* (New York: The Free Press, 1977).

12. For discussion of U.S. military and police aid programs in Vietnam and additional documentation, see: Michael T. Klare, *War Without End: American Planning for the Next Vietnams* (New York: Knopf, 1972), pp. 261-8, 311-64. See also Blaufarb, *The Counterinsurgency Era,* pp. 205-42.

13. Richard Nixon, *U.S. Foreign Policy in the 1970s,* Report to the Congress (Washington, D.C.: Government Printing Office, 1970), pp. 55-6. For discussion, see: Virginia Brodine and Mark Selden, eds., *Open Secret: The Kissinger-Nixon Doctrine in Asia* (New York: Harper and Row, 1972).

14. U.S. Congress, House, Committee on Appropriations, *Foreign Assistance and Related Agencies Appropriations for 1971,* Hearings, 91st Cong., 2d Sess., 1970, p. 307.

15. U.S. Congress, House, Committee on Foreign Affairs, Subcommittee on the Near East and South Asia, *New Perspectives on the Persian Gulf,* Hearings, 93rd Cong., 1st Sess., 1973, p. 39.

16. U.S. Congress, Senate, Committee on Foreign Relations, *Foreign Assistance Authorization, Fiscal Year 1975,* Hearings 93rd Cong., 2nd Sess., 1974, pp. 23-4.

17. U.S. Congress, Senate, Committee on Appropriations, Subcommittee, *Foreign Assistance Appropriations, Fiscal Year 1975,* Hearings, 93rd Cong., 2nd Sess., 1974, p. 1106.

18. Quoted in *The New York Times,* December 12, 1978.

19. U.S. Congress, Senate, Committee on Foreign Relations, *Arms Transfer Policy,* Report to Congress, 95th Cong., 1st Sess., 1977, pp. 26-7.

Chapter 2

1. For background on the history and activities of OPS, see: Klare, *War Without End,* pp. 241-69. See also: Ernest W. Lefever, *U.S. Public Safety Assistance: An Assessment* (Washington, D.C.: Brookings Institution, 1973), pp. 1-26.

2. U.S. Congress, Senate, Committee on Appropriations, *Foreign Assistance Appropriations, 1965,* Hearings, 89th Cong., 2nd Sess., 1964, pp. 72-3.

3. *Survey of the Alliance for Progress,* p. 414.

4. Maxwell D. Taylor, Address to the International Police Academy, Washington, D.C., December 17, 1965, press release, USAID Office of Public Safety.

5. U. Alexis Johnson, "The Role of Police Forces in a Changing World," *Department of State Bulletin* (September 13, 1971), p. 282.

6. "A.I.D. Assistance to Civil Security Forces," press release, USAID Office of Public Safety, Washington, D.C., February 11, 1970.

7. *Ibid.* See also the testimony of David Bell in *Foreign Assistance Appropriations, 1965,* pp. 72 ff.

8. USAID, Office of Public Safety, *Program Guide: Public Safety Training* (Washington, D.C., 1968). See also the quarterly USAID *Operations Report* for data on OPS expenditures and training operations.

9. Jack Anderson in *The Washington Post,* October 8, 1973.

10. USAID, *Program and Project Data Presentation to the Congress,* Fiscal Year 1972 (Washington, D.C., 1971). (Hereinafter cited as: USAID, *Program and Project Data FY72.*)

11. For background on Phoenix, see: U.S. Congress, House, Committee on Government Operations, *U.S. Assistance Programs in Vietnam,* Hearings, 92nd Cong., 1st Sess., 1971. See also: Blaufarb, *The Counterinsurgency Era,* pp. 245-8, 267-9, 274-6; *The Washington Post,* June 18,

1972; *Los Angeles Times,* November 25, 1971; *The Wall Street Journal,* September 5, 1968, and March 25, 1969; and *The New York Times,* October 1, 1969.

12. *U.S. Assistance Programs in Vietnam,* p. 182.

13. *The Washington Post,* June 18, 1972.

14. *U.S. Assistance Programs in Vietnam,* p. 182; additional data from letter from Deputy Assistant Secretary of Defense Dennis J. Doolin to Rep. Jerome Waldie, January 30, 1973.

15. *The Washington Post,* June 18, 1972. See also the testimony of former Phoenix operative K. Barton Osborn in *U.S. Assistance Programs in Vietnam,* and an interview with former Phoenix operative Jeffrey Stein in "From the Ashes, Phoenix," *Commonweal* (April 20, 1973), pp. 154-9.

16. USAID, *Program and Project Data FY72* (and earlier editions). For a full discussion of the OPS program in Thailand, see: Tom Lobe, *United States National Security Policy and Aid to the Thailand Police,* Monograph Series in World Affairs, Graduate School of International Studies (Denver: University of Denver, 1977).

17. U.S. Congress, Senate, Committee on Appropriations, *Foreign Assistance Appropriations for Fiscal Year 1974,* Hearings, 93rd Cong., 1st Sess., 1973, Part I, pp. 1414-18.

18. Letter from William E. Colby to Sen. J. William Fulbright, July 31, 1974. See also: Jack Anderson in *The Washington Post,* August 19, 1974.

19. Amnesty International, *Guatemala: A Government Program of Political Murder* (London: A.I., 1981). For similar information on paramilitary groups in Brazil and Uruguay, see: A.J. Langguth, *Hidden Terrors* (New York: Pantheon, 1978). In his discussion of the U.S. Public Safety Program, Langguth reports that "when Brazilian intelligence officers began to use field telephones to administer electric shocks, it was U.S. agents who informed them of the permissable levels the human body could withstand."

20. U.S. Congress, Senate, Committee on Foreign Relations, *Guatemala and the Dominican Republic,* Staff Memorandum, 92nd Cong., 1st Sess., 1971, p. 6. See also: U.S. Congress, Senate, Committee on Foreign Relations, Subcommittee on Western Hemisphere Affairs, *United States Policies and Programs in Brazil,* Hearings, 92nd Cong., 1st Sess., 1971, and, U.S. Congress, House, Committee on International Relations, Subcommittee on International Organizations, *Torture and Repression in Brazil,* Hearings, 93rd Cong., 2nd Sess., 1974.

21. *Congressional Record* (October 1, 1973), p. S18240.

22. For overviews of U.S. drug programs, see General Accounting Office, *Gains Made in Controlling Illegal Drugs, Yet the Drug Trade Flourishes* (Washington, D.C., October 25, 1979) (hereinafter cited as: GAO, *Gains Made in Controlling Drugs*); U.S. Customs Service, *Updates; Department of State Bulletin,* October 18, 1976; and annual State, Justice, and Treasury Departments' budget requests to Congress.

23. Interview, General Accounting Office, September 6, 1978.

24. Comptroller of the United States, *Stopping U.S. Assistance to Foreign Police and Prisons,* Report to the Congress (Washington, D.C.: GAO, February 19, 1976), p. 22 (hereinafter cited as: GAO, *Stopping U.S. Assistance*).

25. GAO, *Gains Made in Controlling Drugs,* p. 150.

26. U.S. Department of State, *International Narcotics Control, Fiscal Year 1977 Budget,* Congressional Submission, p. 16 (hereinafter cited as: U.S. Department of State, *INC* FY77).

27. U.S. Department of State, *INC,* Fiscal Year 1980, p. 12; U.S. Congress, House, Appropriations Subcommittee on Foreign Operations, *Foreign Assistance and Related Agencies Appropriations for 1979,* Hearings, 95th Cong., 2nd Sess., 1978, Part II, pp. 1178-9.

28. INC memorandum on commodity transfers to Latin America.

29. Comptroller of the United States, *Drug Control in South America Having Limited Success—Some Progress but Problems are Formidable,* Report to the Congress (Washington, D.C.: GAO, March 29, 1978) (hereinafter cited as: GAO, *Drug Control*).

30. U.S. Department of State, *INC,* Fiscal Year 1979, p. 43.

31. *Ibid.,* p. 34.

32. GAO, *Stopping U.S. Assistance,* pp. 22-5.

33. GAO, *Drug Control,* p. 28.

34. "Program of Instruction for International Drug Enforcement Mobile Schools," "Program of Instruction for Advanced International Drug Enforcement School," and "United States Customs Service INC Training Programs": documents received by the authors under the Freedom of Information Act.

35. GAO, *Drug Control,* p. 31.

36. *Ibid.,* p. 31, and U.S. Department of State, Bureau of International Narcotics Matters, *Report to the House Foreign Affairs Committee,* March 1979, received by the authors under the Freedom of Information Act.

37. "Program of Instruction for Specialized Technical Skills Mobile School," document received by the authors under the Freedom of Information Act.

38. Interview, Drug Enforcement Administration, November 20, 1979; and, U.S. Congress, Senate, Committee on Appropriations, *State, Justice, Commerce, the Judiciary and Related Agencies Appropriations for Fiscal Year 1976,* Hearings, 94th Cong., 1st Sess., 1975, Part I, p. 229.

39. U.S. Department of Justice, "Report of June 18, 1975, to the Attorney General (Pursuant to Attorney General's Order No. 600-75, Assigned Employees to Investigate Allegations of Fraud, Irregularity and Misconduct in the Drug Enforcement Administration)," known as the "Defeo Report."

40. Quoted in Carlos Wilson, "The American Connection," *Seven Days* (April 19, 1976), p. 16.

41. Craig Pyes, "Legal Murders," *The Village Voice,* June 4, 1979.

42. "Mexican Connection," *Newsweek,* (April 10, 1978), p. 18.

43. U.S. Catholic Conference, *LADOC* (Washington, D.C., November-December, 1977).

44. U.S. Department of State, Bureau for International Narcotics Matters, *Narcotics Control in Mexico* (Washington, D.C., 1979), pp. 3-8.

45. Quoted in "Mexican Connection," *op. cit.,* p. 18.

46. U.S. Congress, House, Select Committee on Narcotics Abuse and Control, *Oversight Hearings on Federal Drug Strategy,* 95th Cong., 1st

Sess., 1977.

47. "La Operacion CONDOR, Letania de Horrores," *Processo* (Mexico, October 9, 1978), pp. 6-8.

48. Pyes, *op. cit.,* p. 11.

49. *Ibid.,* p. 13.

50. U.S. Department of State, *INC* FY79, p. 33.

51. U.S. Congress, House, Select Committee on Narcotics Abuse and Control, *Southeast Asian Narcotics,* Hearings, 95th Cong., 1st Sess., 1977, p. 10.

52. U.S. Department of State, *INC* FY 79, p. 11.

53. U.S. Congress, House, *Southeast Asian Narcotics, op. cit.,* p. 225.

54. *Ibid.,* p. 220.

55. U.S. Congress, *Conference Report on the Foreign Assistance Act,* 1973.

Chapter 3

1. DSAA, *FMS/MAP Facts 1979,* pp. 17-30; USAID, *U.S. Loans and Grants 1945-79,* p. 6. Unless otherwise noted, all figures on U.S. military aid programs are taken from these two sources.

2. DSAA, *FMS/MAP Facts 1979,* pp. 1-16; DoD, *Security Assistance Program FY81,* pp. 26-31. Unless otherwise noted, all figures on U.S. military sales are taken from these two sources.

3. *Foreign Assistance Act of 1967,* p. 118.

4. DoD, *Security Assistance Program FY81,* p. 16.

5. U.S. Congress, House, Committee on Appropriations, Subcommittee, *Foreign Operations Appropriations for 1963,* Hearings, 87th Cong., 2nd Sess., 1962, Part I, p. 359.

6. From course curricula and other documents supplied to the authors by the Department of Defense under the Freedom of Information Act. For further discussion, see: Klare, *War Without End,* pp. 295-310; Nancy Stein, "The Pentagon's Proteges," *NACLA's Latin America Report* (January, 1976), pp. 3-32; C. Neale Ronning and Willard F. Barber, *Internal Security and Military Power* (Columbus: Ohio State University Press, 1966); and, Miles Wolpin, *Military Aid and Counterrevolution in the Third World* (Lexington, MA: Lexington Books, 1972).

7. *San Francisco Chronicle,* October 10, 1980; *The Washington Post,* October 12, 1980.

8. This discussion is based on: GAO, *Stopping U.S. Assistance.*

9. From "FMS Case Listings" (computerized printout of all FMS transactions) and other data supplied to the authors under the Freedom of Information Act. U.S. arms transfers are also listed in: the *SIPRI Yearbook,* published annually by the Stockholm International Peace Research Institute.

10. For discussion, see: Michael T. Klare, "America's White-Collar Mercenaries," *Inquiry* (October 16, 1978), pp. 14-19; and, Comptroller of the U.S., *Perspectives on Military Sales to Saudi Arabia* (Washington, D.C.: GAO, 1977).

11. See: Jeanne Kirkpatrick, "U.S. Security and Latin America," *Commentary* (January, 1981), pp. 29-40; Ronald Steel, "Are Human Rights

Passe?" *The New Republic* (December 27, 1980), pp. 14-17; and, David R. Griffiths, "Changes Urged to Improve Military Aid," *Aviation Week and Space Technology* (December 15, 1978), pp. 24-5.

Chapter 4

1. From export licenses issued by the Office of Munitions Control to U.S. arms firms; copies obtained by the authors under the Freedom of Information Act. (See Appendix of this book for tabulation of 1976-80 data; for 1973-76 data, see the first edition of *Supplying Repression*.) The concept of the "merchants of repression" was first advanced by Michael Klare and Nancy Stein in: "Merchants of Repression," *NACLA's Latin America Report* (July-August, 1976), pp. 31-2; and, "Exporting the Tools of Repression," *The Nation* (October 16, 1976), pp. 365-70.

2. *London Times,* January 20, 1977.

3. *The Washington Post,* January 22, 1978.

4. *Folha de Sao Paulo,* August 28, 1978.

5. *The Washington Star,* September 20, 1978.

6. *The New York Times,* January 26, 1977.

7. *The New York Times,* May 11, 1968.

8. Telephone interview with Mr. Ken Scheleskey, Cadillac Gage Corp., Warren, Michigan, July 9, 1976. See also: *Jane's Weapons Systems.*

9. Smith & Wesson Academy, course catalog, 1979.

10. *The Washington Post,* November 7 and 22, 1977.

11. See Smith & Wesson advertising supplements in the annual "Buyers Guide" issue (normally in October) of *Police Chief* magazine. On S&W's acquisitions, see the Bangor Punta Corporation's Annual Report for 1968 and subsequent years. Additional documentary information on S&W's aggressive international marketing is contained in the court records of Case C69-177WTS, *Polak, Winters vs. Bangor Punta Corp.,* in the National Archives and Records Center, San Bruno, Calif.

12. Quoted in Richard O. Boyer and Herbert M. Morais, *Labor's Untold Story* (New York: United Electrical, Radio, and Machine Workers of America, 1955), p. 279.

13. Telephone interview with Mr. Henry Wells, Federal Laboratories, Inc., Saltsburg, Pa., September 4, 1976.

14. *The Asian Wall Street Journal,* August 4, 1978.

15. See: *The Wall Street Journal,* October 21, 1976, January 11, 1977; *New Haven Advocate,* October 20, 1976; *The Washington Post,* March 15 and 22, 1978; *The New York Times,* March 14 and 31, 1978; *New Haven Register,* March 15, 1978.

16. Jacobs, Jacobs, and Grudberg, "Memorandum on Behalf of Olin Corporation," memorandum filed in U.S. District Court, New Haven, Conn., March 20, 1978.

17. *The New York Times,* February 27, 1979.

Chapter 5

1. U.S. Department of Commerce, *Export Administration Bulletin, Supplement to Export Administration Regulations* (Washington, D.C.,

December 29, 1977); and U.S. Department of Commerce, Bureau of the Census, *Statistical Classification of Domestic and Foreign Commodities Exported from the United States, Schedule B* (Washington, D.C., 1978).

2. U.S. Department of Commerce, Bureau of the Census, *FT410 Reports* (Washington, D.C., 1976 and later editions).

3. *Ibid.*

4. *Ibid.*

5. Cynthia Arnson, "The Exporting of Torture by America," *Los Angeles Times,* April 26, 1978.

6. "Shok Baton" advertising brochure supplied to the authors by Jonas Aircraft and Arms Co., New York, NY. See also: Amnesty International, *Evidence of Torture* (London: A.I., 1977), pp. 27-31.

7. A.I., *Evidence of Torture,* pp. 29-30.

8. Col. Rex Applegate, "Nonlethal Police Weapons," *Ordnance* (July-August, 1971), pp. 63-4.

9. Letter from Juanita M. Kreps to Michael T. Klare, April 5, 1977.

10. Laurie Nadel and Hesh Weiner, "Would You Sell a Computer to Hitler," *Computer Decisions,* (February, 1977).

11. John Dinges and Saul Landau, *Assassination on Embassy Row* (New York: Pantheon, 1980), pp. 238-9.

12. E Systems Garland Division, "Systems for Industry and Government," (Dallas, TX, 1977), p. 9.

13. E Systems, "E Systems is the Answer," (Dallas, TX, 1977), p. 15.

14. Nadel and Weiner, *op. cit.,* p. 26; see also, "Newsdata," *Computer Decisions* (March, 1977), p. 64.

15. Quoted in *Dallas Times Herald,* April 20, 1978.

16. See Cynthia Arnson and Michael Klare, "Human Rights: Here Is the Noble Theory . . . But is This the Practice, at Least in Brazil?" *Los Angeles Times,* July 2, 1978; and *Police Chief* (October, 1977), p. 121.

17. For discussion, see: U.S. Congress, House Committee on Foreign Affairs, Subcommittee on Africa, *Implementation of the U.S. Arms Embargo,* Hearings, 93rd Cong., 1st Sess., 1973; and, U.S. Congress, House, Committee on International Relations, Subcommittee on Africa, *U.S.-South Africa Relations: Arms Embargo Implementation,* Hearings, 95th Cong., 1st Sess., 1977; and, Maxwell Mehlman, *et al.,* "United States Restrictions on Exports to South Africa," *American Journal of International Law,* Vol. 73, No. 4 (October, 1979), pp. 581-603.

18. Cited in Tad Szulc, "Why Are We in Johannesburg?" *Esquire* (October, 1974), p. 60.

19. U.S. Congress, *U.S.-South African Relations,* p. 56.

20. See: Jennifer Davis, "South Africa's Military Build-Up," *Southern Africa* (December, 1975), pp. 5-9.

21. *The Washington Post,* December 15, 1977.

22. See: *The St. Louis Post-Dispatch,* March 18, 1979; and, *Africa News* (May 25, 1979), p. 11. For discussion, see: Michael T. Klare, "South Africa's U.S. Weapons Connections," *The Nation* (July 28-August 4, 1979), pp. 75-8.

23. *Aviation Week and Space Technology* (July 10, 1978), p. 16; Aviation Advisory Services, *MILAVNEWS* (Essex, England, November, 1979); and John W.R. Taylor, ed., *Jane's All the World's Aircraft* (London,

1976-77), p. 394.

24. See Cynthia Arnson and Michael Klare, "Law or No Law, the Arms Flow," *The Nation* (April 29, 1978).

25. *Ibid.;* Aviation Advisory Services, *MILAVNEWS* (Essex, England, April, 1978), p. 2.

26. *Liberation,* May 22, 1980.

Chapter 6

1. See: *The Washington Post,* November 7, 1978; February 1, 1980.

2. Cynthia Arnson, "In El Salvador: Why Back Regime Based on Violence?" *Los Angeles Times,* December 8, 1980.

3. See: "Castro's Trojan Horses vs. Reagan's Crusaders," *The Washington Post,* December 28, 1980.

4. *The Washington Post,* February 3, 1981.

5. *The Washington Post,* March 15 and 20, 1981.

6. For background on the private security industry, see: James S. Kakalik and Sorrel Wildhorn, *The Private Police Industry: Its Nature and Intent,* Report to the Law Enforcement Assistance Administration by the RAND Corporation (Washington, D.C.: Government Printing Office, 1972). On Intertel, see: Jim Hougan, "A Surfeit of Spies," *Harper's* (December, 1974), pp. 52-66.

7. Quoted in the *Los Angeles Times,* February 21, 1981.

8. The text of the letter, along with a list of signatories was reprinted in *The New York Times,* December 18, 1980.

9. From text in *The New York Times,* June 6, 1980.

10. On South Korea, see: *The Washington Post,* March 16, 1978; and, U.S. Congress, House Committee on International Organizations, *Activities of the Korean Central Intelligence Agency in the United States,* Hearings, 94th Cong., 2nd Sess., 1976. On Iran, see: Richard T. Sale, "SAVAK Said to Work in Washington," *The Washington Post,* May 10, 1977. On Chile, see: John Dinges and Saul Landau, *Assassination on Embassy Row.*

APPENDIX I:

THE INTERNATIONAL REPRESSION TRADE:

- ## SCOPE AND DYNAMICS
- ## SUPPLIERS, RECIPIENTS, COMMODITIES
- ## WHERE TO GO FOR MORE INFORMATION

AUTHOR'S NOTE: The first edition of **Supplying Repression** *appeared at a time when researchers in many countries were becoming interested in the relationship between arms sales and human rights, and it was soon joined by a number of similar studies on the military exports of France, Great Britain, the Netherlands, and several other countries.* As a result of these studies and our own ongoing research on U.S. repression sales, it has become increasingly evident that we are all looking at individual components of what can be best described as the* **international repression trade**—*the global commerce in police weapons, prison gear, intelligence systems, torture devices, and related hardware.** Although the United States is indisputably one of the leading*

---

*These studies include: Centre Local d'Information et de Coordination pour l'Action Non Violente, *Les Trafics d'Armes de la France* (Paris: Maspero, 1977); Pierre Fabre, "Ventes d'Armes - La Politique Francaise," *Alert Atomique* (Paris: Mouvement pour le Desarmement, la Paix, et la Liberte, 1978); Amnesty International, British Section, *The Repression Trade* (London: A.I., 1980); Campaign Against the Arms Trade, *The Arms Traders* (London: CAAT, 1980); Interkerkelijk Verdesberaad, *Nederland in de Wapenhandel* (The Hague: IKV, 1977).

**This concept was first advanced by Michael Klare in "Le Commerce International des Moyens de Repression," *Le Monde Diplomatique* (June, 1979), pp. 18-19; and, "The International Repression Trade," *Bulletin of the Atomic Scientists* (November, 1979), pp. 22-7.

participants in this commerce, it is obvious that we cannot fully appreciate the dynamics of the repression trade unless we view it as an international system with a large supporting cast of manufacturers, traders, and recipients. Thus, while our principal concern remains the U.S. trade in repression technology, we feel that it is essential that we conclude this edition with a brief overview of the larger, worldwide commerce in such hardware.

—M. Klare

SCOPE AND DYNAMICS

No one knows the full extent of the international repression trade. Most governments refuse to provide any information whatsoever on such exports, and the few non-governmental organizations like SIPRI (Stockholm International Peace Research Institute) which publish data on the arms trade usually concentrate on major weapons sales (tanks, missiles, aircraft, etc.) which are easier to track and verify. Researchers seeking to investigate the repression trade must depend, therefore, on individual country data (where available), occasional newspaper reports, trade publications, and other fragmentary documentation. Despite the paucity of information, however, it is possible to map out the broad outlines of this commerce.

For the purpose of analysis, the repression trade can be considered a subdivision of the global arms trade. Many of the producers of conventional weapons also produce arms for the repression trade, and such hardware is usually exported through the same trade channels used for regular military equipment. (In the United States, for instance, police and paramilitary gear are exported along with military gear through the Foreign Military Sales and Commercial Sales programs.) It is important to recognize, however, that the repression trade includes many products which are not normally considered "weapons" at all—such items as riot clubs, thumbscrews, prison gear, and computer systems—but which nevertheless play an important role in political warfare. In addition to such "hardware," moreover, the repression trade also encompasses a wide variety of "software"—training and advisory services, intelligence exchanges, technical assistance, political cooperation, etc. Such exchanges are hard to valuate in dollar terms, but nontheless constitute a major component of the repression trade.

Depending on what is included (i.e., police and security systems only, or paramilitary and counterinsurgency hardware as well), the international repression trade probably amounts to $1-5 billion annually. This may not seem like much when compared to the $25 billion-plus annual trade in conventional military hardware, but when spent on small arms and other light equipment—which cost far less than tanks and other major weapons—this represents a substantial investment in global repression capabilities. And because so many of the countries that acquire this technology are ruled by military juntas or martial-law regimes, this commerce probably has a far greater impact on the day-to-day lives of ordinary people than the more visible and costly trade in military hardware.

As in the case of the larger arms trade, repression sales are motivated by a complementary set of motives involving both supplier and recipient. The "demand side" of the equation is relatively easy to chart: any undemocratic government threatened by popular discontent is likely to import assorted repressive systems for use by its security forces in combatting dissent. In many cases, such action creates a self-sustaining requirement for repression imports, since any increase in state violence is likely to generate an ever-increasing pool of dissidents and thus progressively complicate the task of repression. Ultimately, this can lead to a condition of civil war, wherein the full resources of the state are mobilized in a never-ending struggle to protect the incumbent government against the population at large.* This was the case in Iran and Nicaragua during the final days of the Shah and Somoza, and prevails today in such countries as Afghan-

*For a fuller discussion of this phenomenon, see: Carol Ackroyd, *et al., The Technology of Political Control* (Harmondsworth: Penguin, 1977); and, Marjo Hoefnagels, ed., *Repression and Repressive Violence* (Amsterdam: Swets & Zeitlinger, 1977).

istan, Argentina, El Salvador, Ethiopia, Guatemala, and the Philippines.

The motives on the "supply side" are a little more complex. Money is, of course, a major factor—repression sales can be quite lucrative, especially for the smaller firms which specialize in such weaponry. Money is also the principal motivation for the import-export firms in countries like Belgium, Spain, and Portugal which often serve as "transshipment points" for arms produced elsewhere. For the major powers, however, other motives also prevail: in many cases, these countries wish to ensure the survival of friendly regimes threatened by popular unrest, and thus will actively assist the internal security forces of the government in question. Such support may be motivated by political or ideological considerations (i.e., a desire to protect a trusted ally or co-subscriber to a particular political or religious doctrine), by economic considerations (a desire to retain access to valuable resources or markets on beneficial terms), or security considerations (a desire to ensure cooperation in joint military ventures, or to retain access to key bases). Once a major power perceives a vested interest in the survival of a client, moreover, it is likely to provide ever-increasing quantities of repression hardware (and even, in some cases, military forces) to help overcome its domestic opposition. Thus Washington is providing stepped-up aid to the embattled governments in El Salvador, Thailand, and the Philippines, while Moscow continues to aid the embattled governments in Afghanistan, Angola, and Ethiopia.

Clearly, the international repression trade is fueled by an interlocking set of motives which ensure that supplier nations will look favorably on requests for continuing deliveries to recipient governments. So long as these market forces prevail—and there is nothing to suggest their imminent demise—the repression trade will continue to grow. The long-term results of all this, of course, is that entrenched governments will become more repressive, and that opposition movements will increasingly resort to violence in their efforts to alter the status quo.

SUPPLIERS, RECIPIENTS, COMMODITIES

Having discussed the scope and dynamics of the repression trade, it is useful to list some of the major commodities, suppliers, and recipients involved. This survey should not be considered definitive, but rather as a preliminary audit which requires considerable amplification and expansion. Because data on the repression trade is so scarce, we have only included those entries for which some documentation can be found, and invite our readers to seek additional information and to send us such for future editions of this survey.

COMMODITIES:

Listed below are some of the major weapons, devices, and services provided through the international repression trade.*

Crowd-control systems: Tear-gas grenades, projectiles, and dispensing systems (includes CN, "tear gas"; and CS, "pepper gas"); Chemical "MACE" and similar incapacitating chemical agents; riot batons, shields, and helmets; rubber bullets; water cannon.

Small arms: pistols and revolvers; rifles, carbines, and shotguns; submachine guns.

Police and prison hardware: handcuffs, billy clubs, etc.; leg-irons, chains, shackles, etc.; walkie-talkies and other communications aids.

Torture devices (most such products are home-made, but some items are traded internationally): electronic shock devices; trauma-producing drugs; thumb-screws, truncheons, and saps.

Surveillance devices: night-vision and infra-red scopes; eavesdropping and telephone-tapping equipment; intrusion-detection systems; closed-circuit television.

---

*For more information on these commodities, see: *Jane's Infantry Weapons; Jane's Weapons Systems;* Steve Wright, "New Police Technologies," *Journal of Peace Research*, Vol. 15, No. 4 (1978), pp. 305-22; and Rex Applegate, "Nonlethal Police Weapons," *Ordnance* (July-August, 1971), pp. 62-6.

Data-processing systems: computerized intelligence systems; computerized identification and fingerprint systems; police command, control, and communications systems.

Vehicles: police patrol cars; jeeps and other off-road vehicles; armored cars and internal security vehicles; helicopters.

Counterinsurgency gear: aerial reconnaissance systems; counterinsurgency aircraft (light planes equipped with surveillance gear and armed with rockets, bombs, and napalm); troop-carrying helicopters and transport planes; amphibious vehicles and armored personnel carriers; chemical defoliants; barbed wire.

Training and services: riot-control and firearms training (often provided in conjunction with hardware sales); technical and management assistance; intelligence exchanges and assistance; computer programming and processing; private guard services: electronic security systems management.

SUPPLIERS AND RECIPIENTS:

Given the scarcity of "hard" information on repression sales, it is impossible to provide a detailed breakdown of such transactions such as those compiled on major arms transfers. Nevertheless, the available data allows us to make some general observations about global trading patterns.* Roughly speaking, the participants in the global repression trade can be divided into four main categories:

Major suppliers, which export a full range of repression hardware as part of their larger commerce in military hardware. The five countries in this category— the United States, the Soviet Union, France, Great Britain, and West Germany—account for approximately 80 percent of the world arms traffic and a very large

---

*This survey is largely based on the following sources: *Jane's Infantry Weapons;* the *SIPRI Yearbook; Milavnews* (a private intelligence newsletter published in England); and *The Military Balance* (an annual publication of the International Institute for Strategic Studies in London).

(although probably lower) percentage of world repression sales.

Secondary suppliers and traders, which tend to specialize in the production and sale of small arms, armored cars, and light aircraft. Major producers of such hardware include Belgium, Italy, Switzerland, Canada, Japan, Poland, and Czechoslovakia. Also included in this category are some countries (Belgium, Italy, Spain, Portugal) which serve as international brokers and shippers of military and police hardware.

Third World producers, which manufacture small arms and counterinsurgency gear for their own use and, in some cases, for sale to other countries. This category includes several countries—Israel, South Africa, Taiwan—which have been subject to arms embargoes at one time or another and have therefore developed indigenous military factories. It also includes a number of the wealthier Third World countries (including Argentina, Brazil, China, India, Indonesia, Pakistan, Turkey, and South Korea) which seek to spur modernization and self-sufficiency by developing modern arms industries. Most of these countries produce for their internal market exclusively, but some—notably Israel and Brazil—have become major suppliers of counterinsurgency hardware to other Third World countries.

Recipients, which depend for all or most of their police and security hardware on foreign suppliers. While these countries tend to be more eclectic in their choice of repression suppliers than in their choice of regular arms suppliers (many countries which acquire combat arms from Moscow, for instance, often shop for their police gear in the West), some persistent trade patterns can be detected. Thus the two superpowers tend to be the major providers to their closest allies and clients (the United States to South Korea, Taiwan, the Philippines, Thailand, Indonesia, Saudi Arabia, and the Central American countries; the Soviet Union to North Korea, Vietnam, Ethiopia, Algeria, Afghanistan, Angola, Southern Yemen and the Eastern European countries), while the major European suppliers tend to be persistent suppliers to their former colonies (Great Britain to Kenya, Jamaica, *106* Nigeria, Oman, Bangladesh, Borneo; France to Morocco,

Chad, Gabon, Mauritania). Other recipients, including most of the Latin American countries, tend to avoid the major powers and to buy from secondary suppliers, from Third World producers, or from a combination of sources.

These categories are not airtight, of course, but do provide a rough picture of global supplier/trader/recipient relationships. In presenting this picture, we have heretofore spoken of national entities only; in many countries, however, weapons sales are generally the province of private firms or autonomous state organizations which conduct their own international marketing operations. Because these firms often play a major role in the repression trade, we will complete this picture with a list of some of the major producers and exporters of police and paramilitary hardware. This inventory is by no means complete, but does list many of the major components of what can be called the "international police-industrial complex."*

United States: Smith & Wesson (handguns, shotguns, tear gas, Chemical "MACE," riot clubs, police and prison hardware, firearms training); Federal Laboratories (tear gas, police and prison hardware, riot-control training); Colt Industries (M-16 rifle, handguns); Rockwell International (OV-10 counterinsurgency plane, Printrak-250 fingerprint computer); Technipol Inc. (police and prison hardware, eavesdropping devices); Fargo International (exporters of police and prison hardware); Cadillac-Gage (V-150 armored car); GTE-Sylvania (police communications systems, intrusion detection systems).

United Kingdom: Schermuly Ltd. (CS grenades, riot guns, rubber bullets, police hardware); Marconi (police communications systems, surveillance systems); Ferranti (police communications systems); Short Brothers (Shorland armored car); GKN Sankey (AT-105 armored internal security vehicle); Burroughs (police com-

---

*Entries on this list are derived from the following sources: Steve Wright, "The Police Industrial Complex," in Hoefnagels, ed., *Repression and Repressive Violence, op. cit.,* pp. 161-5; the annual "Police Buyers Guide," in the October issue of *Police Chief* magazine; the *SIPRI Yearbook; Jane's Infantry Weapons;* "Internal Security Equipment," *Defence Materiel* (London, March-April and May-June, 1979).

puters); SAS Group (crowd-control systems).

West Germany: Heckler & Koch (pistols, rifles, submachine guns); Siegfried Peters Electronics (distributors of police hardware and riot-control systems); P.K. Electronics (eavesdropping devices).

France: Panhard (AML-60/90 armored car, M3 armored personnel carrier); Reims-Cessna (F-337 counterinsurgency aircraft).

Soviet Union: State ordnance factories (pistols, rifles, submachine guns, BTR-series armored car, BMP-1 armored car, BRDM-2 armored vehicle).

Belgium: Fabrique Nationale (pistols, rifles, submachine guns, tear-gas grenades, rubber bullets).

Switzerland: MOWAG (Roland, Piranha, and Grenadier armored internal security vehicles).

Italy: Beretta (pistols, revolvers, submachine guns).

Czechoslovakia: Ceskoslovenska Zbrojovka (pistols, rifles, submachine guns).

Israel: Israel Military Industries (Uzi submachine gun).

Brazil: Engesa (EE-9 Cascavel armored car and EE-11 Urutu armored personnel carrier).

(Readers wishing to supply additional entries to this list can write to: Institute for Policy Studies, Militarism & Disarmament Project, 1901 Que St. NW, Washington, D.C. 20009.)

WHERE TO GO FOR MORE INFORMATION

As the relationship between arms sales and human rights has become better understood, more and more religious, humanitarian, and peace organizations have taken an interest in studying—and, in some cases, opposing—the international repression trade. Among the groups which have been most active in this area are:

International:

Amnesty International (International Secretariat: 10 Southampton St., London, WC2, England; U.S. Offices: 304 W. 58th St., New York, NY 10019; 705 G St. S.E., Washington, D.C. 20003; 3618 Sacramento St., San Francisco, CA 94118). Conducts investigations and publishes reports on human rights conditions in selected countries, and organizes campaigns for the release of political prisoners and for the abolition of capital punishment. Recently, A.I. has also begun to focus on the repression trade, and some individual country sections have issued reports and statements on this topic. See: the A.I. *Report on Torture* (1975); the A.I. *Annual Report;* A.I. British Section, *The Repression Trade* (1980).

International Commission of Jurists (B.P. 120, Chene-Bourgeries, 1224 Geneva, Switzerland). Conducts investigations and publishes studies on human rights and judicial procedures in selected countries.

International League for Human Rights (236 E. 46th St., New York, NY 10017). Issues reports on human rights conditions in selected countries and campaigns for public and government awareness of human rights issues. See: *Human Rights Bulletin, Annual Review.*

World Council of Churches (150 Route de Ferney, 1211 Geneva, Switzerland). Supports and coordinates the work of member churches in the areas of human rights, international peace and disarmament, and racial justice.

SIPRI (Stockholm International Peace Research Institute, Sveavagen 166, S11346 Stockholm, Sweden). Maintains a "data base" on international military issues and publishes an annual register of arms transfers. See: *SIPRI Yearbook: International Armaments and Disarmament* (annual).

Campaign Against the Arms Trade (5 Caledonian Rd., London N1, England). Maintains a "data base" on British involvement in the arms trade, and campaigns against military and police sales to Third World countries. See: *CAAT Newsletter* (monthly); *The Arms Traders: Military Exporters in the U.K.* (1980).

Working Group on Armaments and Underdevelopment (IFSH-Arbeitsgruppe, Von Melle Park 15, 2000   *109*

Hamburg 13, West Germany). Maintains a "data base" on international military issues and publishes reports on arms imports and military production in the Third World. See: Peter Lock and Herbert Wulf, *Register of Arms Production in Developing Countries,* (1977).

State Research (9 Poland St., London W1, England). Publishes a critical journal on government security operations in the United Kingdom and other industrialized nations. See: *State Research* (bimonthly).

Project Ploughshares (Conrad Grebel College, University of Waterloo, Waterloo, Ontario, Canada N2L 3G6). Conducts studies and promotes public awareness of disarmament and human rights issues, with an emphasis on Canadian involvement in the arms trade and nuclear arms race. See: *Ploughshares Monitor* (bimonthly); Ernie Regehr, *Making a Killing: Canada's Arms Industry* (Toronto, 1975).

United States:

Coalition for a New Foreign and Military Policy (120 Maryland Ave. N.E., Washington, D.C. 20002). A coalition of peace and human rights organizations which organize grass-roots lobbying campaigns against U.S. support for Third World dictators. See: *Close-Up* (quarterly); *Human Rights Action Guide* (annual).

National Council of Churches (475 Riverside Dr., New York, NY 10027). Supports and coordinates the work of member churches in the areas of human rights, peace and disarmament, and racial justice.

American Friends Service Committee (1501 Cherry St., Philadelphia, PA 19102). Supports and coordinates the work of regional AFSC offices in the areas of human rights, peace and disarmament, and economic and social justice. Also works in coalitions with human rights groups in opposing military aid to Third World dictators. (See also: NARMIC.)

NARMIC (National Action/Research on the Military-Industrial Complex, c/o American Friends Service Committee, 1501 Cherry St., Philadelphia, PA 19102). Maintains a "data base" on military issues and publishes materials on U.S. military sales and operations in the

Third World. See: *Arming the Third World* (1979).

Institute for Policy Studies (1901 Que St. N.W., Washington, D.C. 20009). Maintains a "data base" on international arms transfers and publishes reports on international political, economic, and military issues. See: Klare and Arnson, *Supplying Repression* (1981); D. Volman, *A Continent Besieged: Foreign Military Activities in Africa* (1980); Klare and Volman, *Arms Trade Data* (1981).

Center for National Security Studies (122 Maryland Ave. N.E., Washington, D.C. 20002). Conducts studies on the activities of U.S. intelligence agencies. See: Morton Halperin, *et al., The Lawless State: The Crimes of the U.S. Intelligence Agency* (New York: Penguin, 1976); *First Principles* (monthly); *Intelligence Report* (periodic).

Center for International Policy (120 Maryland Ave. N.E., Washington, D.C. 20002). Conducts studies on the human rights implications of U.S. military and economic aid programs in the Third World. See: *International Policy Report* (bimonthly).

Human Rights Internet (1502 Ogden St. N.W., Washington, D.C. 20010). Publishes biennial directories of organizations and agencies active in international human rights, and a newsletter on human rights activities. See: *North American Human Rights Directory* (1980); *Human Rights Directory: Latin America, Africa, Asia* (1981); *European Directory of Human Rights Organizations* (1981); *Human Rights Research Manual* (1981); *Human Rights Internet Reporter* (bimonthly).

APPENDIX II:

TABLE A:
U.S. Military Aid to Foreign Governments
Fiscal Years 1950-79[1]
(Current U.S. dollars in millions)

Explanatory Notes:

MAP Grants = Grants of arms, equipment, and services under the Military Assistance Program.

FMS Credits = Credits awarded under the Foreign Military Sales Program for the purchase of U.S. arms.

EDA = Deliveries of "surplus" U.S. arms under the Excess Defense Articles Program.

IMET = Training provided under the International Military Education and Training Program.

ESF = Subsidies awarded to threatened pro-U.S. regimes from the Economic Support Fund (formerly known as the Security Supporting Assistance Program).

Region & Country	MAP Grants	FMS Credits[2]	EDA	IMET	ESF[3]	Total
LATIN AMERICA						
Argentina	34.0	175.9	4.4	12.8	19.9	247.0
Bolivia	33.4	23.0	10.1	14.2	164.1	244.8
Brazil	207.2	264.6	83.1	16.5	75.5	646.9
Chile	80.5	62.5	24.0	16.9	—	183.9
Colombia	83.2	105.3	17.9	15.3	31.5	253.2
Costa Rica	0.9	5.0	0.1	0.9	—	6.9
Cuba	8.6	—	5.5	2.0	—	16.1
Dominican Republic	21.7	3.0	3.9	10.6	209.2	248.4
Ecuador	32.0	35.6	10.4	12.6	21.9	112.5
El Salvador	5.0	3.4	2.5	5.8	—	16.7
Guatemala	16.3	10.7	6.7	7.5	33.5	74.7
Guyana	—	—	—	—	9.6	9.6
Haiti	2.4	1.2	0.2	1.3	47.7	52.8
Honduras	5.6	12.5	2.0	8.4	1.6	30.1
Jamaica	1.1	—	*	*	11.0	12.1
Mexico	*	4.3	0.1	2.7	1.2	8.3
Nicaragua	7.7	8.0	5.2	11.5	8.0	40.4
Panama	4.6	3.5	1.7	4.8	27.0	41.6
Paraguay	9.5	0.7	11.2	6.7	—	28.1
Peru	75.0	98.0	20.3	19.5	1.7	214.5
Surinam	—	—	—	—	1.0	1.0
Trinidad & Tobago	—	—	—	—	29.7	29.7
Uruguay	41.0	18.3	20.4	6.6	—	86.3
Venezuela	*	124.6	0.3	14.0	—	138.9
TOTAL	669.7	960.1	230.0	190.6	694.1	2,744.5

Region & Country	MAP Grants	FMS Credits²	EDA	IMET	ESF³	Total
NEAR EAST & SOUTH ASIA						
Afghanistan	*	—	—	5.6	25.4	31.0
Bahrain	—	—	—	—	1.1	1.1
Bangladesh	—	—	—	0.5	—	0.5
Cyprus	—	—	—	—	46.6	46.6
Egypt	—	1,500.0	—	0.6	3,369.7	4,870.3
India	90.4	27.3	22.0	6.3	—	146.0
Iran	766.7	496.4	61.6	67.4	205.3	1,597.4
Iraq	45.2	—	3.3	1.5	—	50.0
Israel	—	11,104.2	—	—	3,554.5	14,658.7
Jordan	467.6	392.8	46.0	9.3	840.7	1,756.4
Lebanon	13.6	76.7	0.3	2.6	20.4	113.6
Nepal	1.7	—	*	0.5	—	2.2
Pakistan	650.3	7.6	26.8	24.6	589.8	1,299.1
Saudi Arabia	23.9	254.2	1.8	12.5	—	292.4
Sri Lanka	3.2	0.3	*	0.3	7.2	11.0
Syria	—	—	—	0.1	438.0	438.1
Turkey	3,136.0	785.0	857.7	111.4	873.6	5,763.7
TOTAL	5,198.6	14,644.5	1,019.5	243.2	9,972.3	31,078.1
EUROPE						
Austria	96.3	15.7	8.2	1.4	—	121.6
Belgium	1,203.8	7.8	21.3	33.9	—	1,266.8
Denmark	587.3	—	20.9	30.5	—	638.7
Finland	—	—	—	0.2	—	0.2

Region & Country	MAP Grants	FMS Credits[2]	EDA	IMET	ESF[3]	Total
France	4,045.1	80.4	289.8	108.0	76.5	4,599.8
Greece	1,681.7	852.5	451.0	46.2	348.9	3,380.3
Iceland	—	—	—	*	24.9	24.9
Italy	2,243.7	0.3	214.6	46.6	—	2,505.2
Luxembourg	7.8	—	0.2	0.5	—	8.5
Malta	—	—	—	—	74.7	74.7
Netherlands	1,178.1	2.2	44.0	39.1	—	1,263.4
Norway	862.2	—	44.1	31.7	—	938.0
Portugal	396.3	—	24.1	18.6	345.0	784.0
Spain	686.8	362.3	82.7	39.1	516.5	1,687.4
United Kingdom	1,012.9	—	73.0	21.6	186.6	1,294.1
West Germany	884.8	—	0.7	16.2	—	901.7
Yugoslavia	689.6	1.4	27.5	4.3	325.5	1,048.3
TOTAL	15,576.4	1,322.6	1,302.1	437.9	1,898.6	20,537.6
EAST ASIA & PACIFIC						
Australia	—	115.6	—	—	—	115.6
Burma	72.1	—	12.3	4.3	9.0	97.7
Indochina	709.0	—	21.9	0.6	777.2	1,508.7
Indonesia	194.7	126.7	33.9	28.0	63.0	446.3
Japan	810.3	34.8	175.0	44.6	—	1,064.7
Kampuchea	1,178.5	—	85.2	14.6	543.3	1,821.6
Laos	1,460.1	—	97.8	42.8	774.0	2,374.7
Malaysia	—	135.9	—	3.7	—	139.6
New Zealand	—	1.5	—	—	—	1.5

Region & Country	MAP Grants	FMS Credits[2]	EDA	IMET	ESF[3]	Total
Philippines	560.2	94.1	98.1	34.4	195.3	982.1
Singapore	—	17.2	—	—	—	17.2
S. Korea	5,129.4	1,084.4	667.5	156.1	2,332.0	9,369.4
S. Vietnam	14,773.9	—	1,100.5	302.1	5,378.5	21,555.0
Taiwan	2,554.2	547.7	941.8	103.2	549.1	4,696.0
Thailand	1,158.2	133.9	243.2	75.0	400.5	2,010.8
TOTAL	28,600.6	2,291.8	3,477.2	809.4	11,021.9	46,200.9
AFRICA						
Algeria	—	—	—	—	1.3	1.3
Botswana	—	—	—	—	26.3	26.3
Cameroon	0.2	7.0	*	*	3.0	10.3
Ethiopia	185.8	36.0	30.2	22.7	3.3	278.0
Gabon	—	6.0	—	—	—	6.0
Ghana	—	—	—	1.1	—	1.1
Guinea	0.8	—	0.1	0.1	22.4	23.4
Ivory Coast	0.1	—	—	0.1	0.3	0.5
Kenya	—	87.0	—	2.3	—	89.3
Lesotho	—	—	—	—	5.5	5.5
Liberia	5.3	8.8	0.4	3.9	5.0	23.4
Libya	12.6	—	2.2	2.8	21.8	39.4
Mali	1.9	*	0.2	1.1	3.5	6.7
Mozambique	—	—	—	—	1.5	1.5
Nigeria	—	0.3	—	1.5	73.0	74.8
Rwanda	—	—	—	—	1.1	1.1

Region & Country	MAP Grants	FMS Credits[2]	EDA	IMET	ESF[3]	Total
Senegal	2.6	8.0	*	0.4	0.1	11.1
Sudan	–	6.3	–	1.4	–	7.7
Swaziland	–	–	–	–	12.8	12.8
Tunisia	40.5	107.5	6.9	5.9	11.6	172.4
Uganda	–	–	–	–	3.0	3.0
Upper Volta	0.1	–	–	0.2	–	0.3
Zaire	23.3	111.0	5.2	9.8	293.5	442.8
Zambia	–	–	–	–	50.0	50.0
TOTAL	273.2	377.9	45.2	53.3	539.0	1,288.7
International Organizations	–	23.1	–	–	–	23.1
WORLD TOTAL	50,318.5	19,620.0	6,074.0	1,734.4	24,125.9	101,872.8

1. Source: U.S. Department of Defense, *Foreign Military Sales and Military Assistance Facts* (Washington, D.C., 1979); and U.S. Agency for International Development, *U.S. Overseas Loans and Grants* (Washington, D.C., 1980).
2. Includes Fiscal Years 1955-79 only.
3. Includes Fiscal Years 1953-79 only.
*Less than $50,000.

TABLE B:
U.S. Arms Sales to Foreign Governments
Fiscal Years 1955-79[1]
(Current U.S. dollars in thousands)

Region & Country	Foreign Military Sales Program (Agreements)	Commercial Sales (Deliveries)[2]
LATIN AMERICA		
Antigua	—	47
Argentina	200,250	82,859
Bahamas	—	107
Barbados	—	91
Belize	—	145
Bermuda	—	491
Bolivia	2,066	4,085
Brazil	289,747	74,460
Cayman Islands	—	399
Chile	190,264	8,760
Colombia	39,591	17,700
Costa Rica	1,530	952
Cuba	4,510	—
Dominica	—	11
Dominican Republic	2,287	2,248
Ecuador	91,554	21,553
El Salvador	3,479	1,995
French Guiana	—	175
Grenada	—	22
Guadeloupe	—	5
Guatemala	32,391	4,908
Guyana	—	187
Haiti	1,290	1,867
Honduras	9,890	3,895
Jamaica	160	840
Martinique	—	13
Mexico	21,648	11,209
Montserrat	—	3
Netherlands Antilles	—	977
Nicaragua	5,340	4,243
Panama	5,261	9,023
Paraguay	735	1,817
Peru	186,345	24,681
St. Christopher-Nevis	—	3
St. Lucia	—	17
St. Vincent	—	4
Suriname	1	81
Trinidad & Tobago	85	428
Turks & Caicos Is.	—	3

Region & Country	Foreign Military Sales Program (Agreements)	Commercial Sales (Deliveries)[2]
Uruguay	19,439	1,415
Venezuela	244,734	45,671
Virgin Islands	—	67
TOTAL	1,352,597	327,471

NEAR EAST & SOUTH ASIA

Region & Country	Foreign Military Sales Program (Agreements)	Commercial Sales (Deliveries)[2]
Abu Dhabi	5,329	8,566
Afghanistan	—	316
Bahrain	147	2,003
Bangladesh	—	1,008
Cyprus	—	279
Egypt	1,630,923	9,352
India	78,420	41,194
Iran	14,672,347	636,192
Iraq	13,152	240
Israel	9,074,874	934,748
Jordan	981,927	17,275
Kuwait	726,854	11,681
Lebanon	70,411	8,590
Nepal	72	56
Oman	2,715	4,832
Pakistan	457,579	25,753
Qatar	—	3,941
Saudi Arabia	30,790,668	405,909
Sri Lanka	4	42
Syria	1	1,383
Turkey	950,959	44,993
Yemen	318,241	39
TOTAL	59,428,470	2,199,938

EUROPE & CANADA

Region & Country	Foreign Military Sales Program (Agreements)	Commercial Sales (Deliveries)[2]
Austria	167,450	18,853
Belgium	1,770,245	143,866
Canada	1,526,711	657,703
Denmark	1,067,823	63,755
Finland	92	9,973
France	391,837	175,785
Gibralter	—	24
Greece	1,713,806	236,404
Greenland	—	13
Iceland	540	688
Ireland	685	1,441
Italy	793,889	571,291
Liechtenstein	—	58
Luxembourg	3,039	10,783
Malta	—	35

Region & Country	Foreign Military Sales Program (Agreements)	Commercial Sales (Deliveries)[2]
Monaco	—	28
Netherlands	2,426,370	218,062
Norway	1,651,304	81,834
Portugal	18,208	13,762
Romania	—	1,378
Spain	1,123,860	181,437
Sweden	111,504	146,333
Switzerland	806,766	57,196
United Kingdom	3,077,611	361,142
U.S.S.R.	—	10
West Germany	7,239,597	725,984
Yugoslavia	15,462	11,209
TOTAL	24,857,758	3,734,305

EAST ASIA & PACIFIC

Region & Country	Foreign Military Sales Program (Agreements)	Commercial Sales (Deliveries)[2]
Australia	2,398,135	120,549
Brunei	10	2,396
Burma	4,274	9,324
French Polynesia	—	361
Fiji	160	4
Gilbert Is.	—	2
Hong Kong	—	34,417
Indochina	8,542	—
Indonesia	212,463	34,129
Japan	1,355,059	799,680
Kampuchea	—	5
Laos	—	4
Macao	—	134
Malaysia	101,888	151,596
Nauru	—	10
New Caledonia	—	467
New Hebrides	—	9
New Zealand	154,737	15,582
Papua New Guinea	—	508
Philippines	196,915	44,234
Singapore	181,848	50,223
South Korea	2,241,678	226,836
South Vietnam	1,167	66
Taiwan	2,114,465	275,960
Thailand	820,981	44,304
Western Samoa	—	2
TOTAL	9,792,323	1,811,933

AFRICA

Region & Country	Foreign Military Sales Program (Agreements)	Commercial Sales (Deliveries)[2]
Algeria	—	1,869
Angola	—	45

Region & Country	Foreign Military Sales Program (Agreements)	Commercial Sales (Deliveries)[2]
Botswana	—	202
Cameroon	5,529	11,994
Central African Republic	—	57
Chad	—	16
Djibouti	—	11
Ethiopia	134,907	1,522
Gabon	2,318	567
Gambia	—	265
Ghana	354	436
Guinea	—	9
Ivory Coast	—	268
Kenya	119,770	6,375
Lesotho	—	4
Liberia	4,531	1,017
Libya	29,595	31,096
Madagascar	—	574
Malawi	—	10
Mali	—	6
Mauritania	—	156
Mauritius	—	129
Morocco	488,842	47,993
Mozambique	—	448
Niger	8	125
Nigeria	38,821	34,217
Senegal	9	273
Seychelles	—	35
Sierra Leone	—	29
South Africa	3,149	18,632
Sudan	320,489	109
Swaziland	—	113
Tanzania	—	2,354
Togo	—	118
Tunisia	86,369	5,860
Uganda	—	464
Upper Volta	—	62
Zaire	73,570	5,435
Zambia	—	589
TOTAL	703,609	86,669
International Organizations	1,094,374	149,034
WORLDWIDE TOTAL	97,229,132	8,309,349

1. Source: U.S. Department of Defense, *Foreign Military Sales and Military Assistance Facts* (Washington, D.C., 1979).
2. Includes Fiscal Years 1971-79 only. Data not available prior to FY 1971.

121

APPENDIX III:

U.S. ARMS SALES TO THIRD WORLD POLICE FORCES, SEPTEMBER 1976-MAY 1979

Includes sales by the following U.S. firms only:

AA: AAI Corp.; Baltimore, MD
BA: Browning Arms; Morgan, UT
CA: Charter Arms; Stratford, CT
CG: Cadillac Gage Co.; Warren, MI
CI: Colt Industries; New York, NY
FC: Federal Cartridge Co.; Minneapolis, MN
FI: Fargo International; Kensington, MD
FL: Federal Laboratories, Inc.; Saltsburg, PA
GO: General Ordnance Equipment Corp.; Pittsburgh, PA
HS: High Standard Sporting Firearms; Hamden, CT
IA: International Armament Corp.; Alexandria, VA
IG: Ithaca Gun Co.; Ithaca, NY

JA: Jonas Aircraft and Arms Co.; New York, NY
JE: Javelin Electronics; Los Angeles, CA
MS: Mine Safety Appliances; Pittsburgh, PA
NA: North American Arms; Freedom, WY
PM: Plainfield Machine Co.; Dunelin, NJ
PW: Polak, Winter and Co.; San Francisco, CA
RA: Remington Arms Co.; Bridgeport, CT
RP: RPB Industries; Atlanta, GA
SI: Sherwood International Export Corp.; Washington, DC
SW: Smith and Wesson; Springfield, MA
VG: Valley Gun Distributors, Inc.; Northridge, CA
WI: Winchester International; New Haven, CT

Quantity	Manufacturer/Product	Exporter	License Date	Recipient
LATIN AMERICA:				
Antigua				
12	FL gas masks	FL	11/76	Commissioner of Police
68	FL tear-gas grenades, proj., cart.	FL	7/77	Commissioner of Police
48	SW gas grenades & proj.	SW	5/78	Commissioner of Police
Bahamas				
50	FL gas masks	FL	9/76	Nassau Police
26,000 rds.	FL .38 special ammo.	FL	12/76	Nassau Police
200	FL CN gas grenades & proj.	FL	5/78	Nassau Police
200	FL CS gas grenades & proj.	FL	5/78	Nassau Police
21	FL CS & HC gas grenades, shells, proj.	FL	6/78	Royal Bahama Police
Belize				
2,000 rds.	SW .38 cal. ammo.	SW	8/77	Belize Police
1	GO Mk-303A Star-tron n.v.s. & lens	SW	8/78	Belize Police
310	FL CS gas grenades	FL	10/78	Commissioner of Police

123

Quantity	Manufacturer/Product	Exporter	License Date	Recipient
Bermuda				
15,000 rds.	RA .38 cal. cart.	RA	9/77	Commissioner of Police
12	FL 1½" gas guns	FL	12/78	Bermuda Regiment
300	FL gas grenade launching cart.	FL	12/78	Bermuda Regiment
6	FL grenade launchers	FL	12/78	Bermuda Regiment
212	FL CS, CN gas grenades	FL	12/78	Bermuda Regiment
5,000 rds.	RA .22 cal. cart.	RA	2/79	Police HQ
14,000 rds.	RA cart. (.223, .38 cal.)	RA	2/79	Police HQ
Bolivia				
50	SW .38 cal. revolvers	SW	5/77	Ministry of Interior
10	SW .357 cal. revolvers	SW	5/77	Ministry of Interior
160	RP MAC#10 9-mm. SMG	RP	*/78	Customs Officers
250	SW .38 cal. revolvers	SW	5/78	Customs Officers
Brazil				
100	FL 37-mm. gas guns	JA	5/76	State Military Police, Sao Paulo
30	CI M-16 rifles	CI	6/76	State Military Police, Sao Paulo
30	CI M-16 rifles	CI	10/76	Sec'y of Public Security, Alagoas
14	SW revolvers	SW	3/77	State Dept. of Criminal Investigation, Sao Paulo
10,000 rds.	FC .38 cal. cart.	JA	3/79	Brazil Confederation de Tiro as Alvo

Quantity	Manufacturer/Product	Exporter	License Date	Recipient
Cayman Islands				
12	SW .38 cal. revolvers	SW	5/78	Police Department
5,000 rds.	SW .38 cal. ammo.	SW	5/78	Police Department
Colombia				
30	HS 12-ga. riot guns	JA	4/76	Military Industry Security Police
395	RP MAC#10 9-mm. SMG	RP	4/77	National Police
370	FC CS gas grenades & proj.	JA	5/77	Bogota Police
1,400	FC CN gas grenades & proj.	JA	5/77	Bogota Police
100	FC gas grenade launcher cart.	JA	5/77	Bogota Police
1,400	SW .38 cal. revolvers	JA	7/77	National Police
2,500	SW .38 cal. revolvers	JA	11/77	National Police
3,408	FL CN gas grenades	FL	11/77	Ministry of Defense, Army Command
2,000	FL CS gas grenades	FL	11/77	Ministry of Defense, Army Command
20	FL Federal Fogger gas dispenser	FL	11/77	Ministry of Defense, Army Command
1,960	FL cannister for gas mask	FL	11/77	Ministry of Defense, Army Command
21,842	FL CN gas grenade & proj.	FL	11/77	Ministry of Defense, Army Command
5,500	FL CS gas grenade & proj.	FL	11/77	Ministry of Defense, Army Command
1,000	SW .38 cal. revolvers	JA	6/78	National Police

125

Quantity	Manufacturer/Product	Exporter	License Date	Recipient
250,000 rds.	FC .30 cal. ammo.	JA	6/78	National Police
1,400	FL CN gas grenades & proj.	JA	6/78	National Police
300	FL CS gas grenades & proj.	JA	6/78	National Police
8,661	FL CN gas grenades & proj.	FL	8/78	Ministry of Defense, Army Command
3,139	FL CS gas grenades	FL	8/78	Ministry of Defense, Army Command
3	JE n.v.s.	FI	1/79	Colombia National Police
50	FL gas masks	FI	1/79	Colombia National Police
50	MS gas dispensers	FI	1/79	Colombia National Police
1,500	SW kits to assemble .38 cal. revolvers	SW	1/79	for assembly under contract with Ministry of Defense
1,500	SW kits to assemble .32 cal. revolvers	SW	2/79	for assembly under contract with Ministry of Defense

Costa Rica

Quantity	Manufacturer/Product	Exporter	License Date	Recipient
2,000 rds.	SW 89-115 JHP ammo.	SW	7/76	For resale to police
200	GO Mk-III Chemical MACE	SW	*/77	For resale to police
4,000 rds.	SW ammo.	SW	10/77	Costa Rica Police
12	SW gas masks	SW	3/78	Banco Central de Costa Rica
150	SW gas grenades & proj	SW	3/78	Ministry of Public Security Adaptacion Social
8,000 rds.	SW .38 cal. ammo.	SW	3/78	Ministry of Public Security Adaptacion Social

Quantity	Manufacturer/Product	Exporter	License Date	Recipient
Ecuador				
1,000	FL ½" cal. gas guns	JA	2/77	National Police
11,135	FL CS gas grenades & proj.	JA	2/77	National Police
1,000	FI Streamer tear-gas dispenser	FI	*/77	Traffic Police
500	FL gas masks	FL	4/77	Ministry of Government
500	FL gas cannisters	FL	4/77	Ministry of Government
1,000,000 rds.	WI .22 cal. ammo.	WI	11/77	National Police
464	SW .38 cal. revolvers	SW	1/78	National Police
6,000 rds.	SW .357 cal. ammo.	SW	1/78	National Police
10	SW M67 gas masks	SW	2/78	Ministry of Interior
100	GO Chemical MACE	SW	3/78	Police Control of Banco Internacional
100	SW .32 cal. revolvers	SW	3/78	Police Control of Banco Internacional
32	SW .32 cal. revolvers	SW	5/78	Banco Central del Ecuador
7	SW .22 cal. revolvers	SW	8/78	Security Dept., Industria Cartonera
550	SW .38 cal. revolvers	SW	10/78	Police General Command
200,000 rds.	WI .32 cal. ammo.	WI	1/79	National Police
100	SW .32 cal. revolvers	SW	3/79	Security Police, Banco Nacional de Fomento
600	SW .38 cal. revolvers	JA	5/79	For use by prison guards, Quito
50,000 rds.	FC .38 cal. ammo.	JA	5/79	For use by prison guards, Quito

Quantity	Manufacturer/Product	Exporter	License Date	Recipient
El Salvador				
24	SW revolvers (9-mm., .22, .38 cal.)	PW	9/76	Security Guards at Banco Hipotecario
18	SW .38 cal. revolvers	SW	9/76	Security guards at Inst. Salvador de Fomento Industrial
300	SW CN gas proj.	SW	10/76	Police
552	SW CS gas. proj.	SW	10/76	Police
4	SW 37-mm. shoulder gas guns	SW	10/76	Police
26	SW .38 cal. revolvers	SW	9/77	Security guards at Banco Central de Reserva
7	SW .38 cal. revolvers	SW	1/78	Postal Security
19	SW .38 cal. revolvers	SW	2/78	Security guards at Banco Internacional de El Sal.
6	SW .38 cal. revolvers	PW	2/78	Security guards at Banco Financiero
12	SW .38 cal. revolvers	PW	4/78	Security guards at Banco de Fomento Agropecuario
14	SW .38 cal. revolvers	PW	5/78	Security guards at Banco Hipotecario
6	SW .38 cal. revolvers	PW	7/78	Security guards at Lopez Laboratory
28	CI pistols & revolvers	CI	12/78	Security Services for Freund, S.A. de C.V.
4	SW .357 cal. revolvers	SW	1/79	Channel 2 Security Personnel

Quantity	Manufacturer/Product	Exporter	License Date	Recipient
5	SW pistols & revolvers	PW	4/79	Banco de Santander y Panama
4	SW .38 cal. revolvers	SW	5/79	Security guards at coffee plantations & warehouses

Guatemala

Quantity	Manufacturer/Product	Exporter	License Date	Recipient
75,000 rds.	FC .45 cal. ammo.	JA	6/76	Police use
100,000 rds.	FC ammo. (9-mm., .380, .45 cal.)	JA	12/76	Police use
12	SW .38 cal. revolvers	SW	12/76	Federacion Nacional de Tiro
12	SW .22 cal. revolvers	SW	12/76	Federacion Nacional de Tiro
75	CI .38 cal. revolvers	CI	1/77	National Police
600	CI .38 cal. revolvers	CI	8/77	National Police
25,000 rds.	FC .38 cal. ammo.	JA	8/77	National Police
167,500 rds.	WI ammo. (.380, .222, .270, .32, .22, .25, .38 cal.)	WI	10/77	Federacion Nacional de Trio con Armas de Caza
65	WI rifles	WI	10/77	Federacion Nacional de Tiro con Armas de Caza
10	SW .38 cal. revolvers	PW	5/78	Police at Credito Hipotecario
6,050,000 rds.	WI ammo. (.22, .25, .32, .38, .380 cal.)	WI	7/78	Ministry of Finance, Gen. Dir. of Internal Revenue
2,500	AA MPG-100 CN gas gren.	AA	10/78	National Police
2,500	AA MPG-120 CS gas gren.	AA	10/78	Federacion Nacional de Tiro
200	SW .38 cal. revolvers	PW	12/78	National Police
15	CI .38 cal. revolvers	CI	3/79	Federacion Nacional de Tiro
15	CI .22 cal. pistols & revolvers	CI	3/79	Federacion Nacional de Tiro
345,400 rds.	WI ammo. (.22, .243, .250, .270, .38 cal.)	WI	3/79	Federacion Nacional de Tiro

Quantity	Manufacturer/Product	Exporter	License Date	Recipient
12	SW .38 cal. revolvers	SW	3/79	Banco Agricola Nacional
30	CI .38 cal. revolvers	CI	4/79	Federacion Nacional de Tiro
25	CI .22 cal. pistols & revolvers	CI	4/79	Federacion Nacional de Tiro
Guyana				
4,000	FL CS grenades & proj.	FL	10/78	Guyana Police Force
Haiti				
1,000 rds.	SW S38-158 JSP ammo.	SW	9/76	Haitian Police
20	SW .38 cal. revolvers	SW	1/79	Haitian Armed Forces
Honduras				
418,000 rds.	SW S38-158 RN ammo.	SW	8/76	Honduras Police & Govt.
2	SW 9-mm. cal. revolvers	SW	5/77	Personal Services by Honduran Govt.
1,400	SW CS gas discharge grenades	SW	7/77	Public Security Force
300	SW CS & CN gas proj.	SW	7/77	Public Security Force
150	SW gas masks	SW	7/77	Public Security Force
4	SW Pepper Fog gas generators	SW	7/77	Public Security Force
230 qts.	SW CS & CN gas formula	SW	7/77	Public Security Force
7	SW .45 cal. revolvers	SW	8/77	Public Security Force (Tegucigalpa)
1	GO Star-tron n.v.s. and adapters	SW	9/77	Public Security Force (Police)
50	SW .38 cal. revolvers	SW	9/77	Customs Officers

Quantity	Manufacturer/Product	Exporter	License Date	Recipient
Jamaica				
100	GO Mk-IV Chemical MACE	SW	5/76	Police Dept.
800	SW #17 CN gas proj.	SW	5/76	Police Dept.
100	SW CS grenades	SW	5/76	Police Dept.
150	SW CN grenades	SW	5/76	Police Dept.
100	SW #12 CS 37-mm. penetrating proj.	SW	5/76	Police Dept.
32	SW #210 shoulder gas gun	SW	5/76	Police Dept.
50	GO Mk-VII chemical baton	SW	5/76	Police Dept.
217,000 rds.	RA .38 cal. cart.	RA	6/76	For Law Enforcement
30,000 rds.	RA .22 cal. cart.	RA	6/76	For Law Enforcement
1	GO Star-tron n.v.s.	SW	10/78	Police Dept.
1,400	FL CN gas grenades & proj.	FL	11/78	Kingston Police
750	SW .38 cal. revolvers	SW	5/79	For Law Enforcement
Martinique				
11	SW .357 cal. revolvers	SW	6/77	National Police
3	SW .38 cal. revolvers	SW	6/77	National Police
3	GO 134C barrier vests	SW	12/77	National Police
Mexico				
4	* M-2 rifles	IA	7/76	State of Chihuahua for law enforcement
12	CI .38 cal. pistols	IA	7/76	State of Chihuahua for law enforcement
4,000	*cart. (.30, .38, .45 cal., 9-mm.)	IA	7/76	State of Chihuahua for law enforcement

Quantity	Manufacturer/Product	Exporter	License Date	Recipient
15	* handcuffs	IA	7/76	State of Chihuahua for law enforcement
22	GO Star-tron lens & acces.	SW	8/76	Naval Secretariat, for coastal surveillance
6	GO Mk-303A rifle mounts	SW	4/77	Naval Secretariat, for law enforcement
2,320	FL CN gas grenades & proj.	FL	6/77	Federal Police, Mexico City
280	FL CS gas grenades	FL	6/77	Federal Police, Mexico City
450	CI .45 cal. pistols	CI	8/77	Federal Police, Mexico City
40	SW CN & CS gas grenades	SW	8/77	Inspector Gen'l of Police Chihuahua
6	SW 37-mm. shoulder gas guns	SW	8/77	Inspector Gen'l of Police Chihuahua
1	SW grenade launcher	SW	8/77	Inspector Gen'l of Police Chihuahua
500	CI M-16 rifles	CI	9/77	Inspector Gen'l of Police Chihuahua
25	CI M-16 carbines	CI	9/77	Inspector Gen'l of Police Chihuahua
1,050	CI M-16 magazines	CI	9/77	Inspector Gen'l of Police Chihuahua
1	GO Star-tron n.v.s. & accessories	SW	11/77	Judicial Police, State of Jalisco
140	SW .38 cal. revolvers	SW	4/78	Direccion General de Policia y Trans.
10	SW 9-mm. cal. pistols	SW	4/78	Direccion Gen. de Pol. y Tran.

Quantity	Manufacturer/Product	Exporter	License Date	Recipient
25	SW .38 cal. revolvers	SW	5/78	Protection of refinery at Cadereyta
1,000 rds.	SW .38 cal. ammo.	SW	5/78	Protection of refinery at Cadereyta
25	SW .38 cal. revolvers	SW	5/78	Protection of refinery at Atzapatzaleo
1,000 rds.	SW .38 cal. ammo.	SW	5/78	Protection of refinery at Atzapatzaleo
50	SW .38 cal. revolvers	SW	5/78	Protection of refinery at Atzapatzaleo
2,000 rds.	SW .38 cal. ammo.	SW	5/78	Protection of refinery at Atzapatzaleo
9	SW .357 cal. revolvers	SW	6/78	State Police of Chihuahua
2,000 rds.	SW .357 cal. ammo.	SW	6/78	State Police of Chihuahua
10	SW .38 cal. revolvers	SW	6/78	Protection of refinery at Pajaritos
1,100	CI .45 cal. pistols	CI	10/78	Sec'y of National Defense
2	GO Mk-700 Star-tron n.v.s.	SW	12/78	Federal Police, Mexico City
55	CI .38 cal. revolvers	CI	3/79	Mexico Inst. of Social Security
1,000	SW Chemical MACE Mk-IV	SW	5/79	Traffic police

Monserrat (West Indies)

Quantity	Manufacturer/Product	Exporter	License Date	Recipient
200	FL CN gas grenades & proj.	FL	8/76	Comm. of Police

Netherlands Antilles

Quantity	Manufacturer/Product	Exporter	License Date	Recipient
60	FI M-17 gas mask	FI	3/77	National Guard Security Force
25	FI #514 CS grenades	FI	3/77	National Guard Security Force

Quantity	Manufacturer/Product	Exporter	License Date	Recipient
78,000	RA cart. (.38, .380 cal.)	RA	11/77	Law enforcement use
5,000	RA .22 cal cart.	RA	9/78	Law enforcement use
98,000	RA cart. (.25, .38, .380 cal.)	RA	9/78	Law enforcement use
20	SW .357 cal. revolvers	SW	12/78	Police Dept.
10	SW .38 cal. revolvers	SW	12/78	Police Dept.
24	SW .38 cal. revolvers	SW	4/79	Criminal Investigation, Dept. of Customs
Nicaragua				
20	WI .22 cal. rifles	WI	5/76	National Guard
50,000 rds.	WI .38 cal. ammo.	WI	6/76	National Guard
3,750,000 rds.	WI .22 cal. ammo.	WI	6/76	National Guard
155,500	WI centerfire ammo.	WI	6/76	National Guard
80	WI .22 cal. rifles	WI	6/76	National Guard
425	SW .38 cal. revolvers	SW	6/76	National Guard
6	SW .38 cal. revolvers	JA	7/76	National Guard
200	FL gas masks	JA	10/76	National Guard
500	FL CS gas grenades	JA	10/76	National Guard
100,000 rds.	FC .38 cal. ammo.	JA	10/76	National Guard
400,000 rds.	FC .22 cal. ammo.	JA	10/76	National Guard
5,000	CI M-16 rifles	CI	10/76	National Guard
5,000	CI bayonets	CI	10/76	National Guard
35,000	CI .30 cal. magazines	CI	10/76	National Guard
850	RA .22 cal. rimfire rifles	RA	11/76	to Nat'l Guard for use by government agency
100	WI .22 cal. rifles	WI	11/76	National Guard

Quantity	Manufacturer/Product	Exporter	License Date	Recipient
2,120,000 rds.	WI ammo. (.22, .25, .357, .45 cal.)	WI	11/76	National Guard
550,000 rds.	WI ammo. (.22, .32, .380 cal.)	WI	4/77	National Guard
185,000 rds.	WI ammo.	WI	4/77	National Guard
16	SW .38 cal. revolvers	JA	7/77	Ministry of National District for police use
1,000 rds.	FC .38 cal. ammo.	JA	7/77	Ministry of National District for police use
4	FC .22 cal. carbines	JA	7/77	Ministry of National District for police use

Panama

Quantity	Manufacturer/Product	Exporter	License Date	Recipient
50,000	FC .380 cal. cart.	JA	4/76	National Guard
16	CG V-150 Commando APC	CG	8/76	National Guard
94,000 rds.	CG 7.62-mm. ammo.	CG	8/76	National Guard
1,000	FL CS & CN gas proj.	JA	11/76	National Guard
218	SW .38 cal. revolvers	SW	6/77	National Guard
10,000 rds.	SW .357 cal. ammo.	SW	6/77	National Guard
5	SW .38 cal. revolvers	SW	1/78	For use by Banco Nacional
30,000 rds.	FC .38 cal. ammo.	JA	3/78	National Guard
150,000 rds.	SW 9-mm. ammo.	SW	6/78	National Guard
650	CI M-16 rifles	SI	8/78	National Guard
2,000	* M-17 gas masks	SI	8/78	National Guard
5,000	* 30 rd. M-16 magazines	SI	8/78	National Guard
200,000 rds.	SW .38 cal. ammo.	SW	9/78	National Guard
200,000 rds.	WI .22 cal. ammo.	WI	1/79	National Guard
600,000 rds.	WI 5.56 cal. ammo.	WI	1/79	National Guard

Quantity	Manufacturer/Product	Exporter	License Date	Recipient
20	SW revolvers	SW	3/79	Security guards, Banco Nacional de Panama
30,000 rds.	SW .38 cal. ammo.	JA	5/79	National Guard

Paraguay

Quantity	Manufacturer/Product	Exporter	License Date	Recipient
48	SW#23 CS 12-ga. piercing proj.	SW	6/76	Cooperativa Policial Ltda.
60,000 rds.	SW .38 special ammo.	SW	6/76	Cooperativa Policial Ltda.
25,000 rds.	SW 9-mm. cal. ammo.	SW	6/76	Cooperativa Policial Ltda.
5,000 rds.	SW .357 magnum ammo.	SW	6/76	Cooperativa Policial Ltda.
12	SW 12-ga. police shotgun	SW	7/76	Police
50,000 rds.	WI 9-mm. ammo.	WI	11/76	Paramilitary police

Peru

Quantity	Manufacturer/Product	Exporter	License Date	Recipient
2,200	SW .38 cal. revolvers	SW	11/76	Civil Guard
580	SW#5 CS blast dispenser gren.	SW	11/76	Civil Guard
100	FL CN gas grenades	JA	12/76	Naval Police
6	SW revolvers	SW	8/77	Civil Guard, Dir. of Services
3,000	FL CN gas grenades	JA	9/77	Civil Guard, Dir. of Services
2,000	FL CN proj.	JA	9/77	Civil Guard
105	FL CN gas grenades	JA	11/77	Civil Guard
10,000	CI .38 cal. revolvers	CI	12/77	Civil Guard
125	SW .38 cal. revolvers	SW	2/78	Policia de Investigaciones
320	SW .38 cal. revolvers	SW	11/78	Civil Guard, Min. of Interior
2,500	CI .38 cal. revolvers	CI	12/78	Civil Guard
2,456	SW .38 cal. revolvers	SW	1/79	Policia de Investigaciones
6	CI .38 cal. revolvers	CI	5/79	Civil Guard

Quantity	Manufacturer/Product	Exporter	License Date	Recipient
St. Kitts				
30	FL CS gas grenades & proj.	JA	12/76	Defense Force
84	FL 12-ga. launcher cart.	JA	12/76	Defense Force
St. Lucia				
50	FL CS gas grenades	FL	9/78	Chief of Police
700 rds.	VG 12-ga. ammo.	SI	3/79	Commissioner of Police
500 rds.	VG .38 cal. ammo.	SI	3/79	Commissioner of Police
St. Vincent				
50	FL CN gas grenades	FL	5/79	Ministry of Home Affairs, Labour, and Tourism
Surinam				
96,000 rds.	WI ammo. (.22, .25, .32, .38 cal.)	WI	1/77	Police
25	SW .38 cal. revolvers	SW	5/77	Surinam Police
24	SW .38 cal. revolvers	SW	8/77	Security at Stichiting Bank
1,000 rds.	SW .38 cal. ammo.	SW	8/77	Security at Stichiting Bank
70	SW 9-mm. cal. revolvers	JA	11/77	Ministry of Justice & Police
10,000 rds.	FC 9-mm. cal. ammo.	JA	11/77	Ministry of Justice & Police
34	SW .38 cal. revolvers	SW	4/79	Surinam Police
Trinidad & Tobago				
7	SW .38 cal. revolvers	SW	6/76	Prison Security Trinidad
200	FL #6003 gas masks	FI	*/76	Riot Control by Police
50	FL #237 CN gas proj.	FI	*/76	Riot Control by Police

Quantity	Manufacturer/Product	Exporter	License Date	Recipient
50	FL #206 CN gas proj.	FI	*/76	Riot Control by Police
50	FL #121 CN gas grenades	FI	*/76	Riot Control by Police
50	FL #112 CN gas grenades	FI	*/76	Riot Control by Police
18	SW Mk-III Chemical MACE	SW	7/77	Prison Security

Turks & Caicos Islands

Quantity	Manufacturer/Product	Exporter	License Date	Recipient
18	FL riot shields	FL	8/76	Chief of Police
148	FL CN gas grenades & proj.	FL	8/76	Chief of Police
2	FL 1½" cal. riot gas guns	FL	8/76	Chief of Police
3	FL grenade launchers	FL	8/76	Chief of Police
50	FL launcher cart.	FL	8/76	Chief of Police
24	FL gas masks	FL	9/76	Chief of Police

Uruguay

Quantity	Manufacturer/Product	Exporter	License Date	Recipient
100,000	RA .38 cal. cart.	RA	6/76	Ministry of Nat'l Defense

Venezuela

Quantity	Manufacturer/Product	Exporter	License Date	Recipient
16,000 rds.	FC .38 cal. ammo.	JA	5/76	Nueva Esparta Police
133	SW .38 cal. revolvers	JA	6/76	Trujillo Police
12,000 rds.	SW .38 cal. ammo.	JA	6/76	Trujillo Police
4	FL grenade launchers	JA	6/76	Trujillo Police
50	FL CS grenades	JA	6/76	Trujillo Police
15	CI pistols & revolvers	CI	6/76	Judicial Police
2	CI .223 cal. rifles	CI	6/76	Judicial Police
123	SW .38 cal. revolvers	SW	6/76	Governacion State Police
2	SW .357 cal. revolvers	SW	6/76	Governacion State Police

Quantity	Manufacturer/Product	Exporter	License Date	Recipient
5	SW 12-ga. police shotguns	SW	6/76	Governacion State Police
260	SW .38 cal. revolvers	SW	6/76	State Police
10	GO Mk-IV Chemical MACE	SW	7/76	Estado Falcon State Police
4	SW 9-mm. cal. revolvers	SW	7/76	D.F. Police
4	SW .38 cal. revolvers	SW	7/76	D.F. Police
2,000	SW 12-ga. launching cart.	SW	7/76	Estado Zulia State Police
600	SW CS gas grenades	SW	7/76	Estado Zulia State Police
2,000	SW .38 cal. revolvers	SW	7/76	Traffic Police, Ministry of Commerce
300	SW 9-mm. cal. revolvers	SW	7/76	Traffic Police, Ministry of Commerce
3,000 rds.	SW S38-158 RN ammo.	SW	7/76	Federal Amazonas Police
200	SW #35 launching cart.	SW	8/76	Federal Amazonas Police
100	SW #15 CS gas grenades	SW	8/76	Federal Amazonas Police
10	SW #34 grenade launchers	SW	8/76	Federal Amazonas Police
60	SW #15 CS gas grenades	SW	8/76	Estado Barinas Police
35	SW #67 gas masks	SW	8/76	Estado Barinas Police
90	GO Mk-IV Chemical MACE	SW	8/76	Estado Barinas Police
30	SW gas mask	SW	8/76	Estado Falcon State Police
96	SW #17 CS gas proj.	SW	8/76	Estado Falcon State Police
10	GO Mk-VII chemical baton	SW	8/76	Estado Falcon State Police
1,000	SW .38 cal. revolvers	SW	9/76	State Police, Military
50	SW 9-mm. cal. pistols	SW	9/76	State Police, Military
100	SW .22 cal. revolvers	SW	9/76	State Police, Military
60	SW #33 grenade launchers	SW	10/76	Metropolitan Police, Caracas
15,000 rds.	WI .22 cal. ammo.	WI	11/76	Judicial Police

Quantity	Manufacturer/Product	Exporter	License Date	Recipient
965,000 rds.	WI centerfire ammo.	WI	11/76	Judicial Police
1,000	CI .38 cal. revolvers	CI	12/76	Judicial Police
8	SW .38 cal. revolvers	PW	12/76	Guards at Banco Nacional de Ahorroy Prestamo
30	SW gas mask	SW	8/76	Estado Falcom State Police
96	SW #17 CS gas proj.	SW	8/76	Estado Falcom State Police
10	GO Mk-VII chemical baton	SW	8/76	Estado Falcom State Police
1,000	SW .38 cal. revolvers	SW	9/76	State Police, Military
50	SW 9-mm. cal. pistols	SW	9/76	State Police, Military
100	SW .22 cal. revolvers	SW	9/76	State Police, Military
60	SW #33 grenade launcher	SW	10/76	Metropolitan Police, Caracas
15,000 rds.	WI .22 cal. ammo.	WI	11/76	Judicial Police
965,000 rds.	WI centerfire ammo.	WI	11/76	Judicial Police
1,000	CI .38 cal. revolvers	CI	12/76	Judicial Police
8	SW .38 cal. revolvers	PW	12/76	Guards at Banco Nacional de Ahorroy Prestamo
100	GO Mk-IV Chemical MACE	SW	1/77	State Police
300	SW CS gas grenades	SW	1/77	State Police
20,000 rds.	SW S38-158 RN ammo.	SW	1/77	State Police
25	CA .38 cal. revolvers	PW	1/77	Security Surveillance & Transport
4	SW .38 cal. revolvers	PW	2/77	Guards at Ministry of Educ.
5	GO Mk-III Chemical MACE	SW	2/77	General Aviation Command
200	FL CS grenades	JA	2/77	Tachira Police
500,000 rds.	WI .38 cal. ammo.	WI	5/77	Traffic Dept.

Quantity	Manufacturer/Product	Exporter	License Date	Recipient
4	WI rifles	WI	6/77	Ministry of Interior, Special Services Div.
1,400	FL CS gas grenades	JA	6/77	Caracas Metro. Police
100	FL 12-ga. shotgun launchers	JA	6/77	Caracas Metro. Police
1,500	SW 12-ga. launching cart.	SW	6/77	Metropol. Police, Caracas
60	SW .38 cal. revolvers	SW	6/77	for resale to personal security service
1,100	CI .38 cal. revolvers	CI	6/77	Judicial Police
100	CI .45 cal. pistols	CI	7/77	Judicial Police
25	FL CS gas grenades & proj.	JA	7/77	General Police Command for demonstration
2,400	SW CS & CN gas gren.	SW	8/77	State Police or govt. personnel
500	SW M-35 launching cart.	SW	8/77	State Police or govt. personnel
50	SW .38 cal. revolvers	SW	8/77	State Police or govt. personnel
500	SW #15 CS gas gren.	SW	9/77	State Police or govt. personnel
38	SW .38 cal. revolvers	SW	9/77	State Police or govt. personnel
50	SW gas masks	SW	9/77	State Police or govt. personnel
60	RP Ingram 9-mm. SMG	FI	9/77	State Police or govt. personnel
236	CI .38 cal. revolvers	CI	9/77	Judicial Police
160	SW #15 CS gas grenades	SW	11/77	State Police or govt. personnel
1,000	SW launching cart.	SW	11/77	State Police or govt. personnel
1,500	SW .38 cal. revolvers	SW	12/77	State Police or govt. personnel
30	RP Ingram 9-mm. SMG	FI	1/78	State Police or govt. personnel
12	SW revolvers	SW	1/78	State Police or govt. personnel
80	SW .38 cal. revolvers	SW	2/78	Police Command, Guarico
500	SW CS gas grenades	SW	2/78	Police Command, Guarico

Quantity	Manufacturer/Product	Exporter	License Date	Recipient
50	SW gas masks	SW	2/78	Police Command, Guarico
24	SW .38 cal. revolvers	SW	4/78	Casa militar for use by State Police
330	CI .38 cal. revolvers	CI	6/78	Judicial Police
330	CI .45 cal. pistols	CI	6/78	Judicial Police
14,300	FL CS gas gren. & proj.	JA	6/78	National Guard
2,400	FL launching cart.	JA	6/78	National Guard
32,960	FL CS gas gren. & proj.	JA	9/78	State Police Depts.
3,566	FL gas masks	JA	9/78	State Police Depts.
670	FL ammo. vests	JA	9/78	State Police Depts.
21,325	FL launching cart.	JA	9/78	State Police Depts.
144	GO Pepper Fog gas generator	SW	9/78	C.A. Venezulana de Industrias Militares, for sale to police
364	SW gas launchers	SW	9/78	C.A. Venezulana de Industrias Militares, for sale to police
200	FL gas masks	JA	10/78	State Police Depts.
200	SW .38 cal. revolvers	SW	12/78	Ministry of Defense
205	SW gas masks	SW	12/78	C.A. Venezulana de Industrias Militares, for sale to police

Virgin Islands

Quantity	Manufacturer/Product	Exporter	License Date	Recipient
2	FL 1½″ cal. gas guns	FL	4/77	Commissioner of Police
2	FL grenade launcher	FL	4/77	Commissioner of Police
175	FL CN gas grenade & proj.	FL	4/77	Commissioner of Police
110	FL CS gas grenade & proj.	FL	11/77	Tortola Police
2	FL 1½″ cal. gas grenades	FL	4/79	Police Dept., Anguilla

Quantity	Manufacturer/Product	Exporter	License Date	Recipient
10	FL CS gas shells	FL	4/79	Police Dept., Anguilla
20	FL CS gas grenades & proj.	FL	4/79	Police Dept., Anguilla

NEAR EAST AND SOUTH ASIA:

Abu Dhabi

Quantity	Manufacturer/Product	Exporter	License Date	Recipient
800	FL CN gas grenades & proj.	FL	10/77	Gen'l Directorate, Police
2,300	SW gas grenades & proj.	SW	4/78	Police, Ministry of Interior
3	SW gas guns	SW	4/78	Police, Ministry of Interior
10	GO Chemical MACE batons	SW	4/78	Police, Ministry of Interior
10	SW gas masks	SW	4/78	Police, Ministry of Interior
140,000 rds.	SW ammo. (9-mm., .38 cal.)	SW	12/78	Ministry of Interior
18	CI M-16 carbines	CI	5/79	Cabinet Office, Deputy Prime Minister
130	SW .38 cal. revolvers	JA	5/79	Dubai Police

Afghanistan

Quantity	Manufacturer/Product	Exporter	License Date	Recipient
10,000 rds.	SW .38 cal. RN ammo.	SW	4/76	Afghan Police Narcotics Sqd.
36	SW .38 cal. revolvers	SW	*76	Afghan Police Narcotics Sqd.

Bahrain

Quantity	Manufacturer/Product	Exporter	License Date	Recipient
30	SW .38 cal. revolvers	SW	11/76	Ministry of Interior
150	SW .38 cal. revolvers	SW	4/77	Ministry of Interior
10,000 rds.	SW ammo.	SW	4/77	Ministry of Interior
100	SW .38 cal. revolvers	SW	10/77	Ministry of Interior

Quantity	Manufacturer/Product	Exporter	License Date	Recipient
6	RA .223 sniper rifles	SI	10/78	Bahrain Police Dept.
2,000	RA .223 hi-velocity ammo.	SI	10/78	Bahrain Police Dept.
400	RA .223 armalite ammo.	SI	10/78	Bahrain Police Dept.
6,000	FL CS gas grenades & proj.	FL	4/79	Bahrain Police Dept.
400	FL gas masks	FL	4/79	Bahrain Police Dept.
Bangladesh				
43	FL 1½" cal. gas guns	FL	5/76	Police Dept.-Dacca
2,000	FL CN gas grenades & proj.	FL	5/76	Police Dept.-Dacca
300	FL CN gas grenades	FL	8/78	Metropolitan Police, Dacca
307	FL gas masks	FL	8/78	Metropolitan Police, Dacca
Cyprus				
900	FL CN gas grenades & proj.	FL	8/76	Govt. Stores Clearing Ofc.
10,000 rds.	SW S38-158 RN ammo.	SW	12/76	Chief of Police, Nicosia
200	SW .38 cal. revolvers	SW	12/76	Chief of Police, Nicosia
500	MS M-17 gas mask	FI	*/76	Police Use
20	FL 1½" cal. riot guns	FL	12/77	Chief of Police, Nicosia
110,000	RA cart. (.32., .38 cal.)	RA	7/78	Ministry of Interior-Law Enf.
100	FL CN gas shells	FL	10/78	Chief of Police, Nicosia
10	GO MK-700 Star-tron n.v.s.	SW	3/79	Cyprus Police
Egypt				
32,500 rds.	SW S38-158 RN ammo.	SW	6/76	Ministry of Interior -Police Dept.
5,500	FL CS gas grenades	JA	7/76	U.A.R. Police

Quantity	Manufacturer/Product	Exporter	License Date	Recipient
9,704	FL CN gas grenades	JA	7/76	U.A.R. Police
50	FL gas masks	JA	8/76	U.A.R. Police
91,000 rds.	FC ammo. (.22, .38 cal.)	JA	10/76	U.A.R. Police
30,000	FL CS gas grenades	JA	4/77	Ministry of Interior -Police Dept.
41,000	FL CN gas gren., proj., cart.	JA	4/77	Ministry of Interior -Police Dept.
15,000	FL CS gas grenades	JA	4/77	Ministry of Interior -Police Dept.
14,000	FL CN gas grenades & proj.	JA	4/77	Ministry of Interior -Police Dept.
250	FL .37-mm. cal. gas guns	JA	4/77	Ministry of Interior -Police Dept.
23	SW .38 cal. revolvers	SW	7/77	Security Dept. Presidency of the Republic
1,500	SW .38 cal. revolvers	JA	7/77	U.A.R. Police
500	SW .38 cal. revolvers	JA	8/77	U.A.R. Police
6,500	FL CS gas grenades	JA	8/77	U.A.R. Police
42	FL CS gas grenades	FL	4/78	Cairo Police test & eval.
380	SW .38 cal. revolvers	JA	6/78	U.A.R. Police
45,000	FC .38 cal. cart.	JA	6/78	U.A.R. Police
32,200	FL CS gas grenades	JA	7/78	U.A.R. Police
3,500	FL grenade launchers	JA	7/78	U.A.R. Police
100	FL 1½" cal. gas guns	JA	7/78	U.A.R. Police
100,000	FC .22 cal. cart.	JA	7/78	Police practice & training
58,000	FC .38 cal. cart.	JA	10/78	U.A.R. Police

Quantity	Manufacturer/Product	Exporter	License Date	Recipient
1,000 rds.	SW 9-mm. ammo.	SW	5/79	Ministry of Home Affairs
16	SW .357 cal. revolvers	SW	6/79	Presidential Security Force
India				
17,000	FL CN gas proj.	FL	9/76	Comm. of Police, Bombay
20	AA MPG-120 CS gas grenades	AA	5/78	Bureau of Police R&D
10	AA MPG-100 CN gas grenades	AA	6/78	Ministry of Home Affairs
10	AA MPG-110 CN/dye grenades	AA	6/78	Ministry of Home Affairs
1	AA L-10 gas grenade launcher	AA	6/78	Ministry of Home Affairs
10	AA C-200 launching cart.	AA	6/78	Ministry of Home Affairs
Iran				
10	SW .22 cal. revolvers	SW	7/76	Bank Markazi, Tehran
30	SW .32 cal. revolvers	SW	12/76	Bank Melli, Tehran
30	FL chemical agent CS	FI	*/76	Riot Control by Police Dept.
6,387	FL #7P CS gas grenades	FI	*/76	Riot Control by Police Dept.
300	FL #519 CS gas grenades	FI	*/76	Riot Control by Police Dept.
5,447	FL #119 CN gas grenades	FI	*/76	Riot Control by Police Dept.
30	FL #280 CN streamer	FI	6/77	Public Security Dept.
20	SW .32 cal. revolvers	SW	7/77	Bank Rahmi, Tehran
3,000	SW .38 cal. revolvers	SW	8/77	Tehran Police
10,000 rds.	WI .38 cal. cart.	PW	8/77	Guards at Counter-Intell. Dept. Tehran
10	MS M-17 gas mask	FI	10/78	National Police
200	FL #119 CN gas grenades	FI	10/78	National Police
600	AA 12-ga. CS barricade shell	FI	10/78	National Police

Quantity	Manufacturer/Product	Exporter	License Date	Recipient
Iraq				
100	SW 9-mm. cal. pistols	SW	7/76	Police, Baghdad
100	SW .357 cal. revolvers	SW	7/76	Police, Baghdad
10	SW .38 cal. revolvers	SW	7/76	Police, Baghdad
100	SW 9-mm. cal. pistols	SW	9/76	Police HQ, Ministry of Interior
100	SW .357 cal. revolvers	SW	9/76	Police HQ, Ministry of Interior
10	SW .38 cal. revolvers	SW	9/76	Police HQ, Ministry of Interior
Israel				
456,250	RA cart. (.222, .38 cal.)	RA	12/76	Israeli Police: training
2,000	FL CS gas grenades	FL	2/77	Ministry of Defense: Tel Aviv
2,000	FL launcher cart.	FL	2/77	Ministry of Defense: Tel Aviv
150	FL CS gas grenades	FL	6/77	Ministry of Defense: Tel Aviv
3,000	FL CS gas grenades & proj.	FL	7/77	Ministry of Defense: Tel Aviv
2,000	FL launcher cart.	FL	7/77	Ministry of Defense: Tel Aviv
100,000	RA .38 cal. cart.	RA	7/77	Israeli Police: training
70	FL grenade launchers	FL	8/77	Ministry of Defense: Tel Aviv
70	FL 1½" cal. gas guns	FL	8/77	Ministry of Defense: Tel Aviv
80	FL CS gas grenades	FL	1/78	Israeli Police
35	FL CS gas grenades	FL	1/78	Ministry of Defense
1,490,000	RA cart. (.22, .38 cal, 9-mm.)	RA	4/78	Israeli Police: training
32	SW .357 cal. revolvers	SW	4/78	Israeli Police: training
8,500	FL CS gas grenades & proj.	FL	7/78	Ministry of Defense: Tel Aviv

Quantity	Exporter	License Date	Manufacturer/Product	Recipient
2,000	FL	7/78	FL launching cart.	Ministry of Defense: Tel Aviv
2,700	FL	8/78	FL CS gas grenades & proj.	Ministry of Defense: Tel Aviv
5	FL	8/78	FL 1½" cal. gas guns	Ministry of Defense: Tel Aviv
340,000	RA	12/78	RA cart. (.22, .38 cal.)	Israeli Police: training
1,000	RA	1/79	RA 30-06 cal. cart.	Israeli Police: training
20	SW	1/79	SW .357 cal. revolvers	Israeli Police
80	FL	2/79	FL CS gas grenades	Prison Authorities, Israeli Police
1,000,000	RA	3/79	RA .38 cal. cart.	Ministry of Defense
60,000	RA	4/79	RA .22 cal. cart.	Ministry of Defense
501,500	RA	4/79	RA cart. (9-mm., .223, .32, .38, .380 cal.)	Ministry of Defense
20	SW	4/79	SW .357 cal. revolvers	Police law enforcement
10,000 rds.	WI	4/79	WI .38 cal. ammo.	Israeli Police
10	SW	4/79	SW .44 cal. revolvers	Police law enforcement
20	SW	4/79	SW .22 cal. revolvers	Police law enforcement
20	SW	4/79	SW .38 cal. revolvers	Police law enforcement
44	SW	4/79	SW 9-mm. pistols	Police law enforcement
300	SW	5/79	SW Chemical MACE Mk-III	Israeli Prison Authority
12	SW	5/79	SW .37-mm. rubber proj.	Israeli Prison Authority
Jordan				
150,000 rds.	SW	9/76	SW S38-158 RN ammo.	Dir. of Public Security
3,000	SW	1/78	SW .38 cal. revolvers	Dir. of Public Security
3	JA	7/78	SW .41 cal. revolvers	Guards at Jordan Kuwait Bank
150 rds.	JA	5/79	WI .41 cal. ammo.	Jordan Kuwait Bank

Quantity	Manufacturer/Product	Exporter	License Date	Recipient
Kuwait				
30	NA .22 cal. derringers	PW	1/77	Ministry of Interior & Defense
1,000 rds.	* .22 cal. ammo.	PW	1/77	Ministry of Interior & Defense
9	FL gas masks	FL	9/77	Ministry of Interior & Defense
15	WI .30 cal. rifle & scopes	FI	3/79	Ministry of Interior & Defense
100,000	* 9-mm. ammo.	FI	3/79	Ministry of Interior & Defense
200	FL CS gas proj.	FI	3/79	Ministry of Interior & Defense
Lebanon				
113	SW .38 cal. revolvers	SW	1/78	Dir. Gen'l of Nat'l Security
5	SW 9-mm. revolvers	SW	1/78	Dir. Gen'l of Nat'l Security
4,500	SW .38 cal. revolvers	SW	5/78	Interior Security Forces
55	SW 9-mm. cal. pistols	SW	6/78	Dir. Gen'l of Nat'l Security
20	SW .38 cal. pistols	SW	6/78	Dir. Gen'l of Nat'l Security
30	SW .357 cal. revolvers	SW	6/78	Dir. Gen'l of Nat'l Security
25	SW .38 cal. revolvers	SW	6/78	Dir. Gen'l of Nat'l Security
10,000 rds.	SW ammo. (9-mm., .38, .357 cal.)	SW	6/78	Dir. Gen'l of Nat'l Security
30	SW .38 cal. revolvers	SW	2/79	Dir. Gen'l of Nat'l Security
10	SW .357 cal. revolvers	SW	2/79	Dir. Gen'l of Nat'l Security
10	SW 9-mm. cal. revolvers	SW	2/79	Dir. Gen'l of Nat'l Security
10,000 rds.	SW ammo. (9-mm., .38, .357 cal.)	SW	2/79	Dir. Gen'l of Nat'l Security
400	SW revolvers (9-mm., .38, .357 cal.)	SW	5/79	Dir. Gen'l of Nat'l Security
50,000 rds.	SW ammo. (9-mm., .38, .357 cal.)	SW	5/79	Dir. Gen'l of Nat'l Security
Nepal				
14	FL gas masks	FL	5/77	Katmandu Police

149

Quantity	Manufacturer/Product	Exporter	License Date	Recipient
14	FL 1½" cal. gas guns	FL	5/77	Katmandu Police
150	FL CS gas grenades & proj.	FL	5/77	Katmandu Police
75	FL CN gas proj.	FL	5/77	Katmandu Police
Oman				
80	FL 1½" cal. gas guns	FL	12/77	Royal Oman Police
13,000	FL CS gas proj.	FL	12/77	Royal Oman Police
80	FL 1½" cal. gas guns	FL	12/78	Royal Oman Police
100	CI M-16 rifles	SI	3/79	Oman Research Dept.
30,000 rds.	*5.56-mm. ammo.	SI	3/79	Oman Research Dept.
Pakistan				
710	FL CS proj.	FL	6/76	Karachi Police
2,920	FL CS proj.	FL	7/76	Karachi Police
20	FL grenade launchers	FL	7/76	Karachi Police
400	FL launcher cart.	FI	7/76	Karachi Police
970	SW .38 cal. revolvers	SW	8/76	Airport Security Police, Karachi
49,000 rds.	SW .38 cal. ammo.	SW	8/76	Airport Security Police, Karachi
10	SW .37-mm. gas guns	SW	12/77	Superin. Police, Baluchistan
460	SW CS gas grenades & proj.	SW	12/77	Superin. Police, Baluchistan
1,400	SW .37-mm. gas proj.	SW	2/78	Superin. Police, Baluchistan
400	SW CS gas grenades	SW	3/79	Peshawar Police
1,250	SW CS 37-mm. shells	SW	3/79	Peshawar Police
2	GO Mk-V Chemical MACE	SW	3/79	Peshawar Police

Quantity	Manufacturer/Product	Exporter	License Date	Recipient
1,230	SW .37-mm. CS proj.	SW	3/79	Karachi Police
1,250	FL CS gas proj.	FL	4/79	Peshawar Police
Qatar				
10	CI pistols	CI	7/77	Police HQ
100,000 rds.	SW .38 cal. ammo.	SW	5/78	Qatar State Police
600	SW .38 cal. revolvers	SW	5/78	State Police
26	SW revolvers (.357, .44, .45 cal.)	SW	5/78	State Police
10	SW .38 cal. revolvers	SW	3/79	Qatar Police
Saudi Arabia				
20	SW revolvers (.22, .38 cal.)	SW	11/76	Chief of Public Security, Riyadh
30,000 rds.	SW S38-158 JHP ammo.	SW	11/76	Ministry of Interior, Special Security Forces
3,200	SW .38 cal. revolvers	SW	*/76	Ministry of Interior
6	SW .38 cal. revolvers	SW	3/77	Security Protection for Prince Mohamed
50	SW .357 cal. revolvers	SW	7/77	Commander Special Security Forces, Min. of Interior
50	SW .38 cal. revolvers	SW	7/77	Commander Special Security Forces, Min. of Interior
50,000 rds.	SW .38 cal. ammo.	SW	12/77	Public Sec. Directorate, Min. of Interior
10,000	SW .38 cal. revolvers	SW	6/78	Ministry of Interior
500	SW 9-mm. cal. pistols	SW	6/78	Special Security Forces

Quantity	Manufacturer/Product	Exporter	License Date	Recipient
250,000 rds.	SW 9-mm. ammo.	SW	6/78	Special Security Forces
500	SW .38 cal. pistols	SW	7/78	Ministry of Interior
Sri Lanka				
25,000 rds.	SW S38 ammo.	SW	6/76	Colombo Police
16	FL 1½" cal. gas guns	FL	11/78	Colombo Police
500	FL 1½" cal. launching cart.	FL	11/78	Colombo Police
Syria				
72	SW revolvers (9-mm., .22, .32, .357, .38, .41 cal.)	SW	7/77	Command of Interior Security Forces
Turkey				
1,000	SW .38 cal. revolvers	SW	12/77	National Police
2,000	SW .38 cal. revolvers	SW	5/79	National Police
EAST ASIA & PACIFIC				
Brunei				
*	GO 303 n.v.s. w/135 mm. lens	SW	7/76	Brunei Police Dept.
4,800 rds.	WI 5.56 cal. ammo.	WI	9/78	Dept. of Sec. & Intell.
100	CI M-15 rifles	SI	11/78	Govt. Security Office
50,000 rds.	CI 5.56-mm. cal. ammo.	SI	11/78	Govt. Security Office
150,000 rds.	VG .22 cal. ammo.	SI	4/79	Commissioner of Police

Quantity	Manufacturer/Product	Exporter	License Date	Recipient
Fiji				
12	FL CN gas grenades	FL	6/78	Law Enforcement
4	FL CN gas grenades	FL	8/78	Law Enforcement
1	SW Mk-30319 Star-tron n.v.s.	SW	3/79	Royal Fiji Police
Hong Kong				
500	SW CS grenades	SW	8/76	Royal Hong Kong Police
192	FL 1½" cal. gas guns	FL	8/76	Law enforcement duties
1,000	SW CS 37-mm. proj.	SW	8/76	Royal Hong Kong Police
500	SW Mk-II CS gas proj.	SW	9/76	Royal Hong Kong Police
30,000	RA .38 cal. cart.	RA	2/77	Macau Security force-training
2,000	FL baton shells	FL	5/77	Hong Kong Police
500	SW Mk-IV Chemical MACE	SW	8/77	Royal Hong Kong Police
6,000	FL CS gas grenades & proj.	FL	11/77	Hong Kong Police
2,000	FL baton shells	FL	11/77	Hong Kong Police
17	SW Pepper Fog gas generator	SW	2/78	Prisons Staff Training Inst.
70	SW irritant fog formula	SW	2/78	Prisons Staff Training Inst.
134	SW Chemical MACE	SW	2/78	Prisons Staff Training Inst.
180	SW gas shells	SW	2/78	Prisons Staff Training Inst.
700	GO Mk-IV Chemical MACE	SW	8/78	Hong Kong Police
13,000	FL CS gas grenades & proj.	FL	9/78	Hong Kong Police
1,860,000 rds.	WI pistol ammo.	WI	9/78	Hong Kong Police
3,000	FL baton shells	FL	9/78	Hong Kong Police
60	SW CS grenades	SW	10/78	Prisons Dept. Staff Training Institute
53	SW Chemical MACE	SW	10/78	Prisons Dept. Staff Training Institute

Quantity	Manufacturer/Product	Exporter	License Date	Recipient
1	SW Pepper Fog gas generator	SW	10/78	Prisons Dept. Staff Training Institute
500	GO Chemical MACE	SW	*	Police HQ
2,050	CI .38 cal. revolvers	CI	11/78	Hong Kong Police
64	FL 1½" cal. gas guns	FL	12/78	Hong Kong Police
1,000	FL baton shells	FL	5/79	Law enforcement duties, Hong Kong volunteers

Indonesia

Quantity	Manufacturer/Product	Exporter	License Date	Recipient
463	SW crowd control items	SW	8/76	Indonesian Police
100	GO Mk-VII chemical batons	SW	8/76	Indonesian Police
1,366,777 rds.	WI centerfire ammo.	WI	6/77	National Police
250,000	* 8-rd. clips for M-1 rifles	IA	9/78	Dept. of Defense & Security
5	GO Star-tron Mk-303A n.v.s.	SW	12/78	Indonesian Police
435	SW gas masks	SW	1/79	Dept. of Police
15,000	CI M-16 rifles	CI	2/79	Dept. of Defense & Security
60,000	CI 30-rd. magazines	CI	2/79	Dept. of Defense & Security
15,000	CI M-7 bayonets w/scabbards	CI	2/79	Dept. of Defense & Security
1,326	CI .38 cal. revolvers	CI	6/79	Dept. of Defense & Security
64	SW #210 gas guns	SW	7/79	Dept. of Police
500	SW 12-ga. launching cart.	SW	7/79	Dept. of Police
300	SW #98 CS riot agent	SW	7/79	Dept. of Police
500	SW .38 cal. launching cart.	SW	7/79	Dept. of Police

Macao

Quantity	Manufacturer/Product	Exporter	License Date	Recipient
40,000	RA .38 cal. cart.	RA	4/77	Security Force
554	SW .38 cal revolvers	JA	7/78	Police

Quantity	Manufacturer/Product	Exporter	License Date	Recipient
Malaysia				
2,000	SW gas grenades	SW	7/76	Central Police Store
3,900,000 rds.	WI centerfire ammo.	WI	7/76	Police training
4,140	GO Mk-IV Chemical MACE	PW	7/76	Royal Malay Police
15,000	FL CN gas grenades	FL	7/76	Royal Malay Police
1,000	FL launcher cart.	FL	8/76	Kuala Lumpur Police
700	SW .38 cal. revolvers	SW	8/76	Royal Malay Police
20,000 rds.	FC .357 cal. ammo.	JA	9/76	Inspector Genl. of Police
2,000,000 rds.	WI centerfire ammo.	WI	10/76	Royal Malay Police
1,552	FL CS gas grenades	FL	10/76	Kuala Lumpur Police
236	FL #201-Z riot guns	FI	12/76	Malaysian Police
8,000	FL 1½" cal. CN gas shells	FI	12/76	Malaysian Police
4,000	FL 1½" cal. CS gas shells	FI	12/76	Malaysian Police
53	SW .38 cal. revolvers	SW	12/76	Royal Malay Police
5	SW .38 cal. revolvers	SW	1/77	Royal Malay Police
36	SW .38 cal. revolvers	SW	3/77	Securicor security personnel
20	SW .38 cal. revolvers	PW	7/77	Nat'l Bureau of Investigation
5,500,000 rds.	WI 9-mm. ammo.	WI	8/77	Royal Malay Police
15,525	CI M-16 rifles w/bayonets	CI	9/77	Ministry of Home Affairs (Internal Security Forces)
60,900	CI 30-rd. magazines	CI	9/77	Ministry of Home Affairs (Internal Security Forces)
4,000,000	RA .38 cal. cart.	RA	11/77	Royal Malay Police
300	FL 1½" cal. gas guns	FL	1/78	Police, Kuala Lumpur
49,298	FL CN gas grenades & proj.	FL	1/78	Police, Kuala Lumpur
22,764	FL CS gas grenades & proj.	FL	1/78	Police, Kuala Lumpur

Quantity	Manufacturer/Product	Exporter	License Date	Recipient
16,070	SW .38 cal. revolvers	PW	3/78	Royal Malay Police
23	SW .38 cal. revolvers	SW	3/78	for safeguarding Port Kelang by Security Authority
8	CG V-150 Commando APC	CG	3/78	Ministry of Home Affairs
10,389	CI M-16 rifles w/bayonets	CI	5/78	Ministry of Home Affairs (internal security forces)
41,556	CI 30 rd. magazines	CI	5/78	Ministry of Home Affairs (internal security forces)
136	CI telescopes	CI	5/78	Ministry of Home Affairs (internal security forces)
4,000	*M-17 gas masks	SI	6/78	Police Dept.
12,000	FL CS gas grenades & proj.	FL	6/78	Ministry of Defense
609,400 rds.	WI 9-mm. ammo.	WI	7/78	Royal Malay Police
15	AA gas grenades	AA	7/78	Royal Malay Police
2,000	FL CN gas streamer	FL	8/78	Ministry of Home Affairs, Police Div.
63	SW .38 cal. revolvers	JA	1/79	Customs Officers
10	SW .32 cal. revolvers	PW	4/79	State Govt. of Selangor

Papua New Guinea

Quantity	Manufacturer/Product	Exporter	License Date	Recipient
112	FL CN cart. billy	FL	12/77	Royal P.N.G. Constabulary
1	GO Mk-XII Pepper Fog generator	SW	12/77	Royal P.N.G. Constabulary for riot control and training
32 qt.	GO CN & CS gas formula	SW	12/77	Royal P.N.G. Constabulary for riot control & training
6	GO Mk-VII Chemical MACE baton	SW	12/77	Royal P.N.G. Constabulary for riot control and training

Quantity	Manufacturer/Product	Exporter	License Date	Recipient
3	GO Mk-VI,V Chemical MACE	SW	12/77	Royal P.N.G. Constabulary for riot control and training
10,000 rds.	FC .38 cal. ammo.	JA	6/78	Royal P.N.G. Constabulary
20	AA CS gas grenades	AA	6/79	Police use: riot control
Philippines				
200,000	FC .38 cal. primed cases	JA	8/76	Police & other govt. agencies
Singapore				
90,000 rds.	SW S38-158 RN .38 ammo.	SW	4/76	Security Guard Service
17	SW .38 cal. revolvers	SW	6/76	Singapore Customs Offices
12	FL CN gas cart.	FL	6/76	Singapore Police
90	SW .38 cal. revolvers	SW	7/76	Singapore Central Narcotics Bureau
1,000 rds.	SW S38-158 RN ammo.	SW	8/76	Singapore Central Narcotics Bureau
850	SW .38 cal. revolvers	SW	9/76	Singapore Police
3	FL flush formulation	FI	11/76	Singapore Police
3,608,000 rds.	WI pistol ammo.	WI	12/76	Singapore Police
6	FL 1½" cal. gas guns	FL	1/77	Singapore Police
30	FL CN gas cart.	FL	2/77	Singapore Police
110	SW .38 cal. revolvers	SW	2/77	Singapore Police
500	MS M-17 gas masks	FI	7/77	Police use
12	FL CN gas grenades	FL	8/77	Singapore Police
28	FL 1½" cal. riot guns	FL	9/77	Singapore Police
858	FL CN gas grenades & proj.	FL	9/77	Singapore Police
12	SW .38 cal. revolvers	SW	9/77	Singapore Customs Officers

Quantity	Manufacturer/Product	Exporter	License Date	Recipient
4	SW .38 cal. revolvers	SW	9/77	Security Guards, CIS chartered Indus. of Singapore
500	FI #206 CN gas proj.	FI	10/77	Police use
500	FL #506 CS gas proj.	FI	10/77	Police use
6	FL CN gas cart.	FL	10/77	Singapore Police
26	SW .38 cal. revolvers	SW	11/77	Singapore Prison HQ
662	SW .38 cal. revolvers	SW	12/77	Singapore Police Armament
550,000 rds.	WI pistol ammo.	WI	12/77	Singapore Police
2,000	* M-17 gas masks	SI	12/77	Singapore Police
16	GO Mk-XII Pepper Fog generators	SW	6/78	Singapore Police
128 qts.	GO Pepper Fog formula	SW	6/78	Singapore Police
192 qts.	GO gas formula	SW	6/78	Singapore Police
1	GO Pepper Fog generator	SW	6/78	State Police
20 qts.	GO CS & CN Pepper Fog formula	SW	6/78	State Police
874	FL CN gas proj. & cart.	FL	6/78	Singapore Police
784	FL CS gas proj.	FL	6/78	Singapore Police
45	FL #39 blast billy	FL	6/78	Singapore Police
	FL 1½" cal. gas guns	FL	7/78	Director of Prisons
8	SW .38 cal. revolvers	SW	7/78	Singapore Customs Officers
204,000 rds.	WI pistol ammo.	WI	8/78	Singapore Auxiliary Police
65,000 rds.	SW .38 cal. ammo.	SW	10/78	Commercial & Industrial Security Corp., Nat'l Stadium: Customs & Excise Dept.
450	SW .38 cal. revolvers	SW	10/78	Commercial & Industrial Security Corp., Nat'l Stadium: Customs & Excise Dept.
2,000	SW .38 cal. revolvers	SW	1/79	Commercial & Industrial Security Corp., Nat'l Stadium: Customs & Excise Dept.
24 qts.	GO Pepper Fog mix	SW	3/79	Singapore Police

Quantity	Manufacturer/Product	Exporter	License Date	Recipient
5	SW .38 cal. revolvers	SW	3/79	Auxiliary Police: Chartered Industries
1,385,500 rds.	WI .38 cal. ammo.	WI	3/79	Singapore Police
81,000 rds.	WI 9-mm. cal. ammo.	WI	3/79	Singapore Police
South Korea				
44	PM M-2 automatic carbines	JA	10/76	Police use
80	PM M-2 .30 cal. carbines	JA	11/76	Police use
5,000 rds.	WI .357 cal. ammo.	WI	5/77	Presidential Security Force to protect VIPs
250	PM M-2 automatic carbines	JA	8/77	Police use
201	SW .38 cal. revolvers	SW	1/78	Presidential Security Force to protect VIPs
Tahiti				
25	GO Mk-V Chemical MACE w/holster	SW	6/76	Tahiti Police
Taiwan				
950,000 rds.	SW S38-158 RN ammo.	SW	6/76	Police use
3,600	SW .38 cal. revolvers	SW	6/76	Police use
240	GO Mk-IV Chemical MACE	SW	2/77	Inspectorate Gen'l of Customs
2,000 rds.	SW S38-158 RN ammo.	SW	3/77	Nat'l Police Admin.
3,600	SW .38 cal. revolvers	SW	2/78	Min. of Interior, Dept. of Police
420,000 rds.	SW .38 cal. ammo.	SW	2/78	Min. of Interior, Dept. of Police
4,000	FL CN gas proj.	FL	2/78	Law enforcement duties, Chemical Service

Thailand

Quantity	Manufacturer/Product	Exporter	License Date	Recipient
2,500,000 rds.	WI .22 cal. ammo.	WI	5/76	Royal Thai Police
23	SW .357 cal. revolvers	JA	6/76	Police use
6	SW .44 cal. revolvers	JA	6/76	Police use
50,000 rds.	WI centerfire ammo.	WI	8/76	Police shooting range, Bangkok
1,000	SW CS gas grenades	SW	8/76	Thai Police
3,004	SW CS blast disp. grenades	SW	8/76	Bangkok Police
154	SW .357 cal. revolvers	SW	4/77	Police Cadet Academy
2,000	CI bayonets for M-16 rifles	CI	8/77	Royal Thai Police & Police Border Patrol
2,000	CI M-16 rifles	CI	8/77	Royal Thai Police & Police Border Patrol
3,000,000	WI pistol primers	WI	8/77	Royal Thai Police
150,000 rds.	WI pistol ammo.	WI	6/78	Police Dept., Bangkok
25	AA CS grenades & proj.	AA	6/78	Border Patrol Police HQ, Bangkok
1	AA L-110 grenade launcher	AA	6/78	Border Patrol Police HQ, Bangkok
373	SW .357 cal. revolvers	SW	6/78	Police Cadet Academy
286	SW .37-mm. CN proj.	SW	6/78	Police Cadet Academy
300,000 rds.	WI .22 cal. ammo.	WI	12/78	Ministry of Defense
300,000 rds.	WI .22 cal. ammo.	WI	12/78	Ministry of Defense
270	* .30 cal. carbines	SI	3/79	Police Dept., Bangkok
100,000 rds.	WI .38 cal. ammo.	WI	4/79	Ministry of Defense
146	SW .38 cal. revolvers	SW	4/79	Bangkok Police

Quantity	Manufacturer/Product	Exporter	License Date	Recipient
AFRICA				
Algeria				
20	SW .38 cal. revolvers	PW	11/76	Directorate of Nat'l Security Algiers
1,000	SW .38 cal. revolvers	PW	11/77	Directorate of Nat'l Security Algiers
Botswana				
13	CI .38 & .357 cal. revolvers	CI	11/76	Commissioner of Police
1,300 rds.	CI .38 cal. ammo.	CI	11/76	Commissioner of Police
70,000 rds.	WI 5.56-mm. ammo.	WI	1/77	Commissioner of Police
500	FL CS gas proj.	FL	1/78	Commissioner of Police
Gabon				
1	GO Star-tron n.v.s.	SW	12/76	Presidential Guard
Gambia				
4	FL 1½" cal. gas guns	FL	1/79	Banjul Police
Ghana				
5,000	FL CN gas grenades & proj.	FL	11/78	Accra Police
Kenya				
100	GO Mk-V Chemical MACE	SW	*	Police Dept. resale to Sec. Org. & Law Enf. Officers

Quantity	Manufacturer Product	Exporter	License Date	Recipient
170	GO Mk-V reload cart.	SW	*	Police Dept. resale to Sec. Org. & Law Enf. Officers
300	FL CS grenades	FL	8 77	Mombasa Police
25	GO Mk-V Chemical MACE	SW	10 77	Police Dept.
300	GO Mk-V Chemical MACE	JA	2 78	Police & security organizations

Lesotho

Quantity	Manufacturer Product	Exporter	License Date	Recipient
100	FL CS gas grenades	*	3 78	Commissioner of Police

Liberia

Quantity	Manufacturer Product	Exporter	License Date	Recipient
50	FI Mk-III Chemical MACE	FI	7 76	Security Forces
125	FI Mk-V Chemical MACE	FI	7 76	Security Forces
50	FI RDA .32 cal. revolvers	FI	7 76	Security Forces
2	BA 9-mm. pistol	FI	7 76	Security Forces
20,000 rds.	BA ammo.	FI	7 76	Security Forces
13,000	BA pistols	FI	7 76	Security Forces
17	CI .38 cal. revolvers	CI	6 77	Bureau of Immigration & Naturalization
1,000 rds.	CI .38 cal. ammo.	CI	6 77	Bureau of Immigration & Naturalization
30,000	JA .38 cal. cart. case	FI	7 78	Special Security Service
10	* PM30P MZ carbines	FI	9 78	National Police
2,000 rds.	* .30 cal. carbine ammo.	FI	9 78	National Police
10	IG Ithaca 12-ga. shotguns	FI	9 78	National Police
500	*12-ga. #4 buckshot shells	FI	9 78	National Police
5	* 12-ga. shotgun grenade launcher	FI	9 78	National Police
500	* 12-ga. #4 shotgun gren. cart.	FI	9 78	National Police

Quantity	Manufacturer/Product	Exporter	License Date	Recipient
10	FL #201-Z 1½″ cal. gas guns	FI	9/78	National Police
44	CI .22 & .38 cal. revolvers	CI	1/79	Nat'l Public Safety Institute
75	CI .357 & .38 cal. revolvers	CI	1/79	OAU Security Office
235	CI .38 cal. revolvers	CI	1/79	Bur. of Immigration & Naturalization
350	CI .38 cal. revolvers	CI	1/79	National Police
60	CI .38 & .357 cal. revolvers	CI	1/79	Special Security Service
155,000 rds.	WI .357 & .38 cal. ammo.	WI	3/79	Deputy Min. of State in charge of National Security
25,000 rds.	WI .38 cal. ammo.	WI	4/79	Ministry of Justice
59	CI .38 & .357 cal. revolvers	CI	4/79	Ministry of Justice
320	CI .38 cal. revolvers	CI	5/79	Director of Police
110	CI .357 cal. revolvers	CI	5/79	Director of Police

Malta

Quantity	Manufacturer/Product	Exporter	License Date	Recipient
100	SW .38 cal. revolvers	JA	4/77	Commissioner of Police

Mauritius

Quantity	Manufacturer/Product	Exporter	License Date	Recipient
300	FL CN gas proj.	FL	2/77	Port Louis Police
72	FL CS gas pellets	FL	2/77	Port Louis Police
10	FL 1½″ cal. gas guns	FL	3/77	Port Louis Police
80	FL CN gas streamer	FL	2/77	Port Louis Police
3	FL 1½″ cal. riot guns	FL	2/77	Port Louis Police
200	FL CN gas streamer	FL	1/78	Port Louis Police
20	FL 1½″ cal. gas guns	FL	5/78	Port Louis Police
400	FL gas streamer	FL	5/78	Port Louis Police
200	FL CN gas streamer	FL	1/79	Port Louis Police

Quantity	Manufacturer/Product	Exporter	License Date	Recipient
Morocco				
100	CI M-16 carbines	CI	7/78	Nat'l Security Police of Morocco
Nigeria				
42	FL gas proj., grenades, shells	FL	8/77	Nigerian Police
300	SW M-67 gas masks	SW	5/78	Nigerian Prisons Dept.
20,000	FL CS gas proj.	FL	6/78	Nigerian Police
2	SW Mk-303A n.v.s.	FI	12/78	Nigerian Police
210	FL 1½″ cal. gas gun	FL	4/79	Nigerian Police
68,000	FL CS gas proj.	FL	4/79	Nigerian Police
Senegal				
8	SW revolvers	SW	3/79	Dakar Police
Seychelles				
15	SW .38 cal. revolvers	SW	8/76	Police HQ
5,000 rds.	SW S38-90 JSP ammo.	SW	8/76	Police HQ
5,000 rds.	SW JSP ammo.	SW	9/77	Police HQ
1	JE 22T n.v.s.	FI	4/79	Police HQ
Swaziland				
2	SW .32 cal. revolvers	SW	7/76	Commissioner of Police
Tanzania				
2	SW 357 cal. revolvers	SW	4/78	For use by Executive Protection Div. of Security Forces

Quantity	Manufacturer/Product	Exporter	License Date	Recipient
1,000 rds.	SW .357 cal. ammo.	SW	4/78	For use by Executive Protection Div. of Security Forces

Tunisia

Quantity	Manufacturer/Product	Exporter	License Date	Recipient
190	SW .38 cal. revolvers	FI	1/77	National Guard
25,000 rds.	SW .38 spl 110 gr. ammo.	FI	1/77	National Guard
50	FL Federal #210 CN proj.	FI	1/77	National Guard
15,000 rds.	* .45 cal. SMG ammo.	FI	1/77	National Guard
100,000	* .38 cal. pistol primers	FI	1/77	National Guard
1,900	MS M-17 gas masks	FI	7/78	National Guard
5,000	FL gas grenades	FI	7/78	National Guard
7,500	FL spedeheat gas proj.	FI	7/78	National Guard
120	FL #201-Z gas guns	FI	7/78	National Guard
2,000	SW .38 cal. revolvers	SW	8/78	Ministry of Interior
175	SW .38 cal. revolvers	FI	9/78	Palace Guard
2	SW Mk-700 Star-tron n.v.s.	SW	5/79	Ministry of Interior
50	SW Mk-III Chemical MACE	SW	7/79	Ministry of Interior
10	SW barrier vests	SW	7/79	Ministry of Interior

IPS PUBLICATIONS

Research Guide to Current
Military and Strategic Affairs
By William M. Arkin

The first comprehensive guide to public information sources on the U.S. military establishment. Soviet and other foreign military affairs, and global strategic issues. Provides descriptions of all basic research tools. Topics include: the U.S. military defense policy and posture; the defense budget; arms sales and military aid; weapons systems; NATO arms control and disarmament; and intelligence operations. Indispensable for anyone interested in current military and strategic affairs. $15.95 (paper, $7.95).

Real Security: Restoring American
Power in a Dangerous Decade
By Richard J. Barnet

"*Real Security* is a *tour de force,* a gift to the country. One of the most impassioned and effective arguments for sanity and survival that I have ever read."—Dr. Robert L. Heilbroner

"An inspired and inspiring achievement . . . a first salvo in the campaign to turn our current security policies—diplomatic, military, and economic—in the direction of rationality. It may well be the basic statement around which opponents of unalloyed confrontation can gather. It will have great impact."—John Marshall Lee, Vice Admiral, USN (Ret.)

"As a summary of the critical literature on the arms race, Barnet's brief essay is an important antidote to hawkish despair."—*Kirkus Reviews*

$10.95 (paper, $4.95)

The Counterforce Syndrome: A Guide
to U.S. Nuclear Weapons and Strategic Doctrine
By Robert C. Aldridge

This study discloses the shift from "deterrence" to "counterforce" in U.S. strategic doctrine. A thorough, newly-revised summary and analysis of U.S. strategic nuclear weapons and military policy including descriptions of MIRVs, MARVs, Trident systems, cruise missiles, and M-X missiles in relation to the aims of a U.S. first-strike attack. $4.95.

Dubious Specter:
A Skeptical Look at the Soviet Nuclear Threat
By Fred Kaplan

Do the Soviets really threaten American ICBMs with a devastating surprise attack? Will Soviet military doctrine lead the Russians to threaten nuclear war in order to wring concessions from the West? Do Soviet leaders think they can fight and win a nuclear war? Fred Kaplan separates the myths from the realities about U.S. and Soviet nuclear stockpiles and strategies and provides the necessary background for understanding current debates on arms limitations and military costs. $4.95.

The Rise and Fall of the 'Soviet Threat':
Domestic Sources of the Cold War Consensus
Alan Wolfe

A timely essay demonstrating that American fear of the Soviet Union tends to fluctuate according to domestic factors as well as in relation to the military and foreign policies of the USSR. $4.95.

Soviet Policy in the Arc of Crisis
By Fred Halliday

The crescent of nations extending from Ethiopia through the Arab world to Iran and Afghanistan has become the setting of an intense new geopolitical drama. In this incisive study, Halliday reviews the complex role played there by the Soviet Union—a role shaped as much by caution as by opportunity, as much by reaction to American moves as by Soviet initiative. Above all, the Soviet role is defined and limited by the indigenous politics of the region. $4.95.

Beyond the Vietnam Syndrome:
U.S. Interventionism in the 1980s
By Michael T. Klare

A study of the emergence of a new U.S. interventionist military policy. Shows how policymakers united to combat the "Vietnam Syndrome"—the public's resistance to American military involvement in future Third World conflicts—and to relegitimate the use of military force as an instrument of foreign policy. Includes a close look at the Pentagon's "Rapid Deployment Force," and a study of comparative U.S. Soviet transcontinental intervention capabilities. $4.95.

Feeding the Few:
Corporate Control of Food
By Susan George

The author of *How the Other Half Dies* has extended her critique of the world food system which is geared towards profit not people. This study draws the links between the hungry at home and those abroad exposing the economic and political forces pushing us towards a unified global food system. $4.95.

The Nicaraguan Revolution:
A Personal Report
By Richard R. Fagen

Tracing the history of the Nicaraguan Revolution, Fagen focuses on six legacies that define current Nicaraguan reality: armed struggle; internationalization of the conflict; national unity; democratic visions; death, destruction and debts; and political bankruptcy. This primer on the state of Nicaraguan politics and economics provides an insightful view of the Sandinist quest for power and hegemony. The report contains twenty photographs by Marcelo Montecino and appendices with the basic documents necessary for understanding contemporary Nicaraguan affairs. $4.00.

Decoding Corporate Camouflage:
U.S. Business Support for Apartheid
By Elizabeth Schmidt
Foreword by Congressman Ronald Dellums

By exposing the decisive role of U.S. corporations in sustaining apartheid, this study places highly-touted employment "reforms" in the context of the systematic economic exploitation and political repression of the black South African majority.

" . . . forcefully presented."—*Kirkus Reviews*. $4.95.

Postage and Handling:
All orders must be prepaid. For delivery within the USA, please add 15% of order total. For delivery outside the USA, add 20%. Standard discounts available upon request.

Please write the Institute for Policy Studies, 1901 Que Street, N.W., Washington, D.C. 20009 for our complete catalog of publications and films.